Cogs, Gears and Chains
to Color
35 Grayscale Images

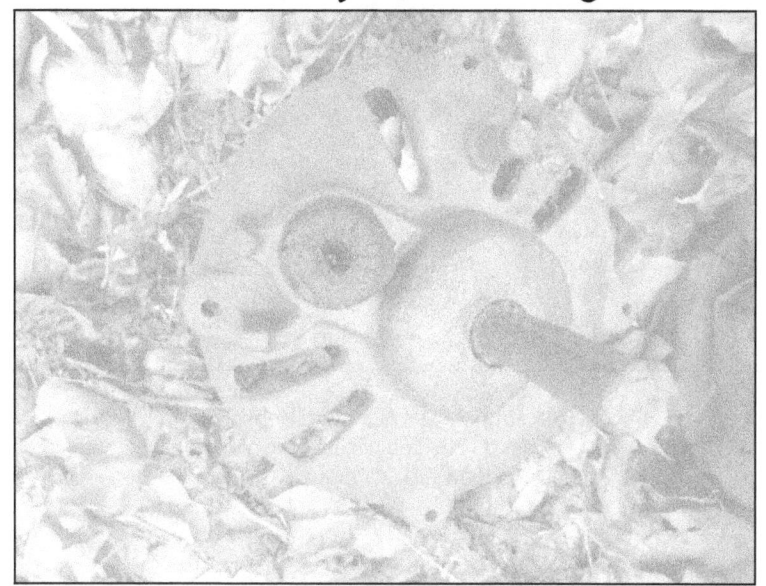

Adult Coloring Book

GRACE BRANNIGAN

Photographs Elaine Warfield

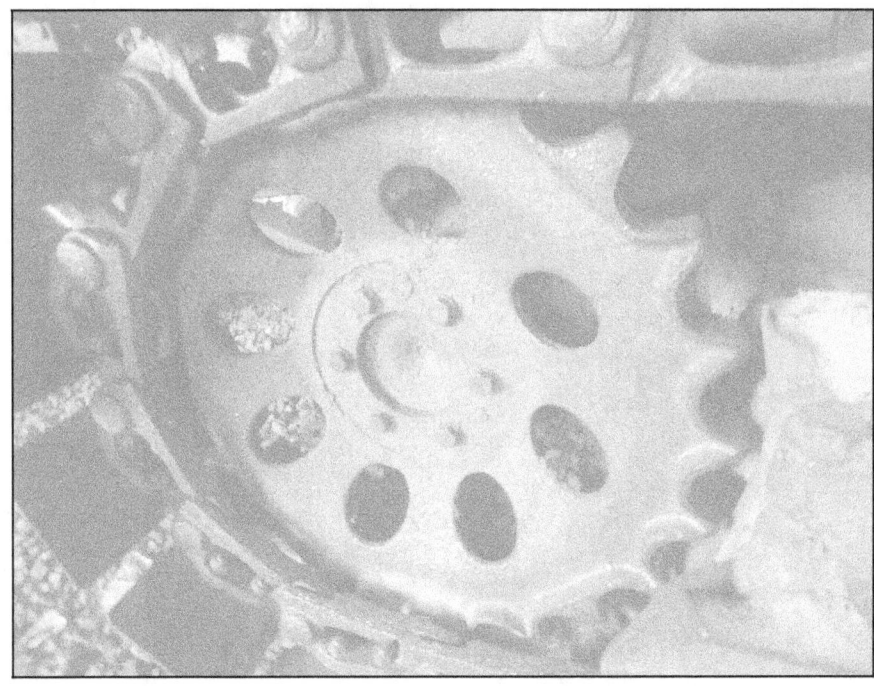

Author Website: http://www.ColoringBooksForAdults.info
Cogs, Gears and Chains to Color
Copyright 2016 Elaine Warfield
ISBN-13- 978-1530274444
ISBN-10: 1530274443

Please check out my other coloring books:

Detailed Mandala Coloring Books 1 through 4
Detailed Alphabet Coloring Book: 25 Baroque Grayscale Images
Renaissance Masks: 25 Grayscale Images
On the Go Pocket Size Coloring Books
Fairies in the Garden
Be My Valentine: Vintage Valentines to Color
Scenic Catskill Mountains: 25 Photographs to Color
and 40+ sketchbooks and journals

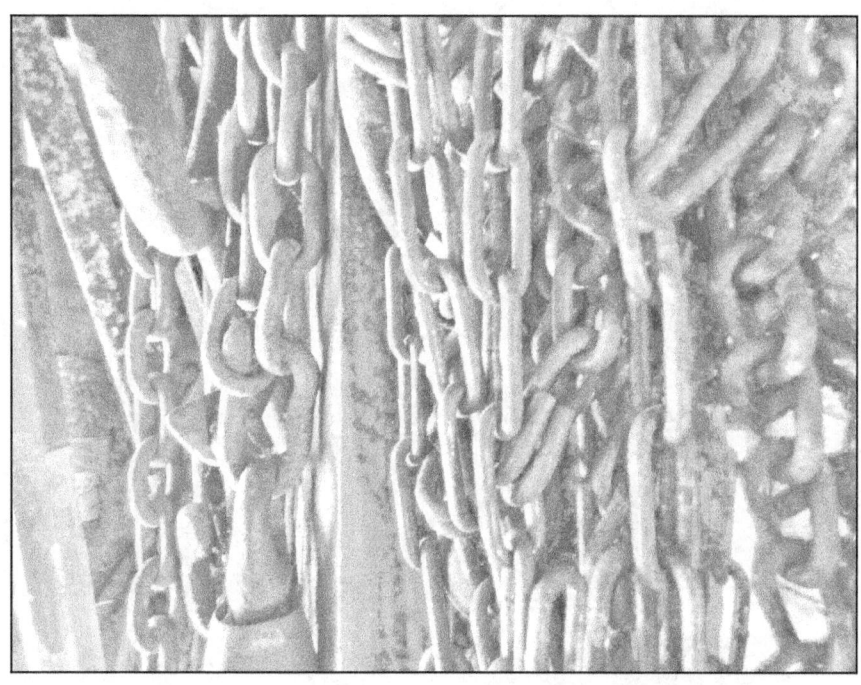

Meditation for the Brain. Allow coloring to soothe you.

This coloring book has 35 Grayscale images for your coloring pleasure! All kinds of Wheels, Gears, Cogs, Chains and more! To give you the optimum coloring experience, most of the images have been rotated to give you the largest space to color!

∞ ∞ ∞ ∞ ∞ ∞ ∞ ∞ ∞ ∞ ∞ ∞ ∞ ∞ ∞ ∞

How to Color Grayscale: Coloring *Grayscale* images is a fun way to explore and color and it makes shading easier to learn when you follow the shading already in the images. The end result is a uniquely rich and rewarding colored image. Use permanent markers, gel pens and watercolor pencils. Experiment, have fun!

Coloring has been shown to reduce stress and offer meditative release. Create your own visually appealing art using crayons, colored pencils, felt tip markers, ink pens, art pencils, gel pens, glitter pens. There is no limit to your creativity and genius.

Please leave a review where you bought this coloring book and share your coloring images. It really helps the author and other buyers. Please check out my other coloring books and visit my Facebook page **Coloring Books for Adults Info.**

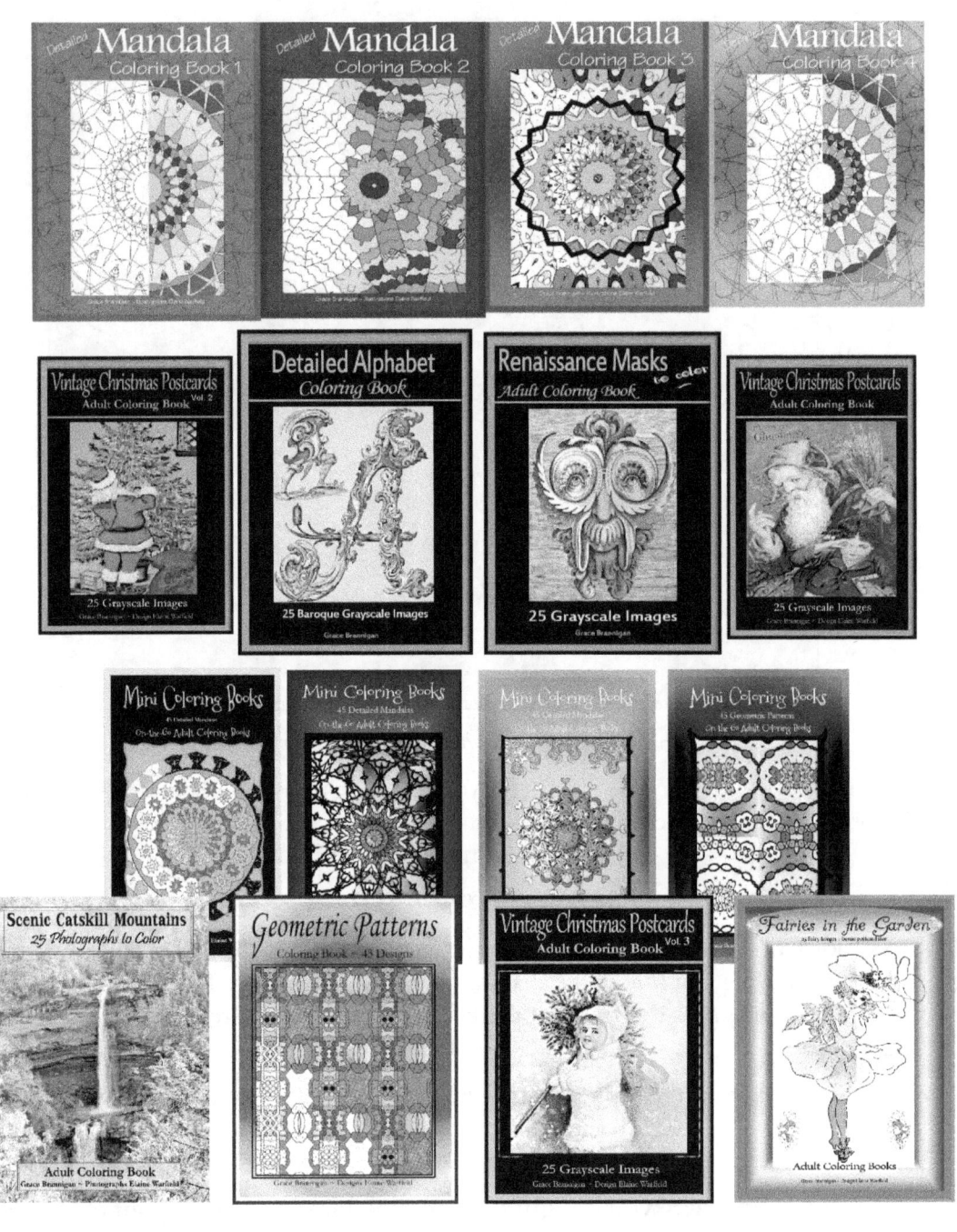

Color, Color, Color!

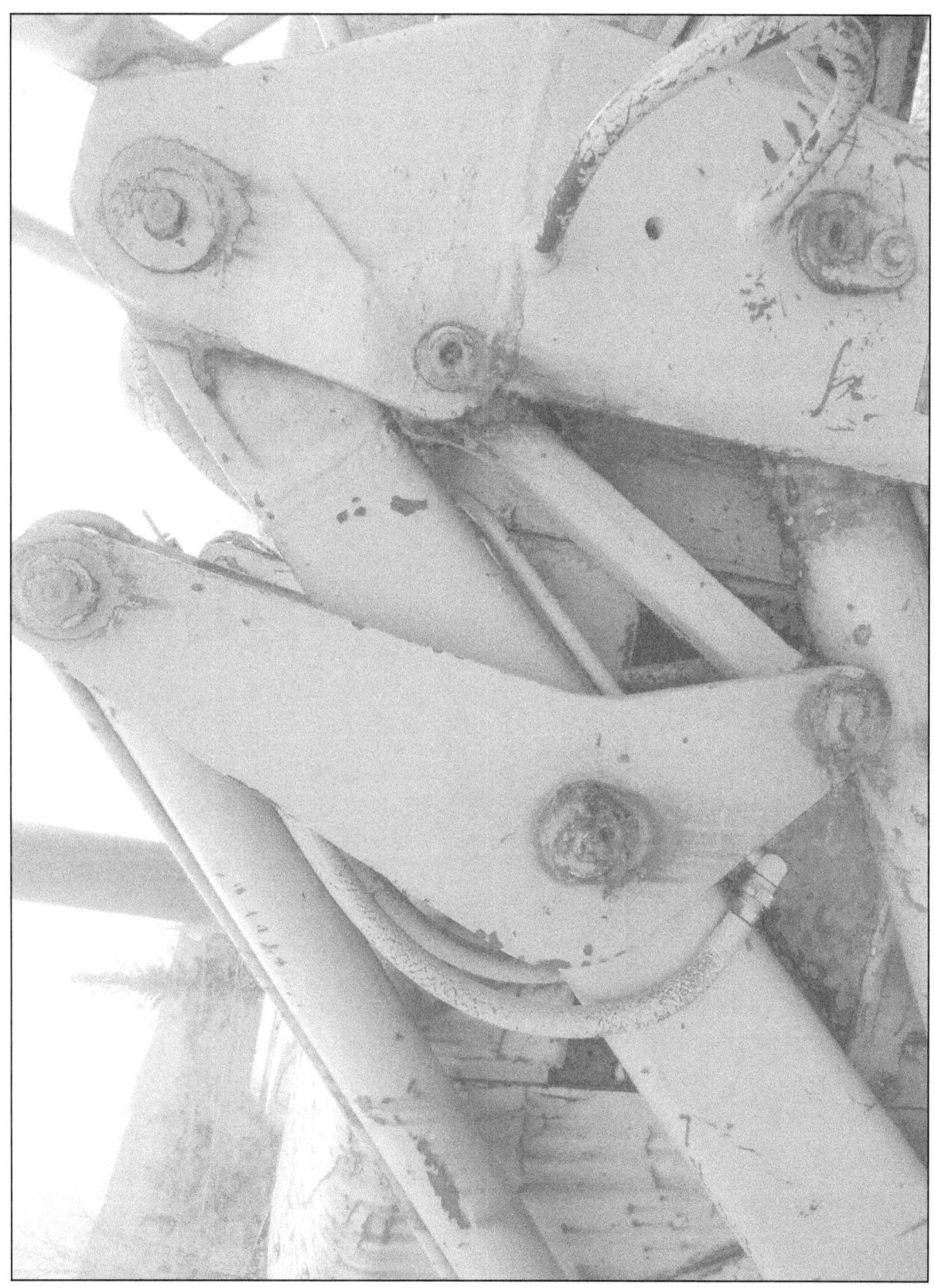

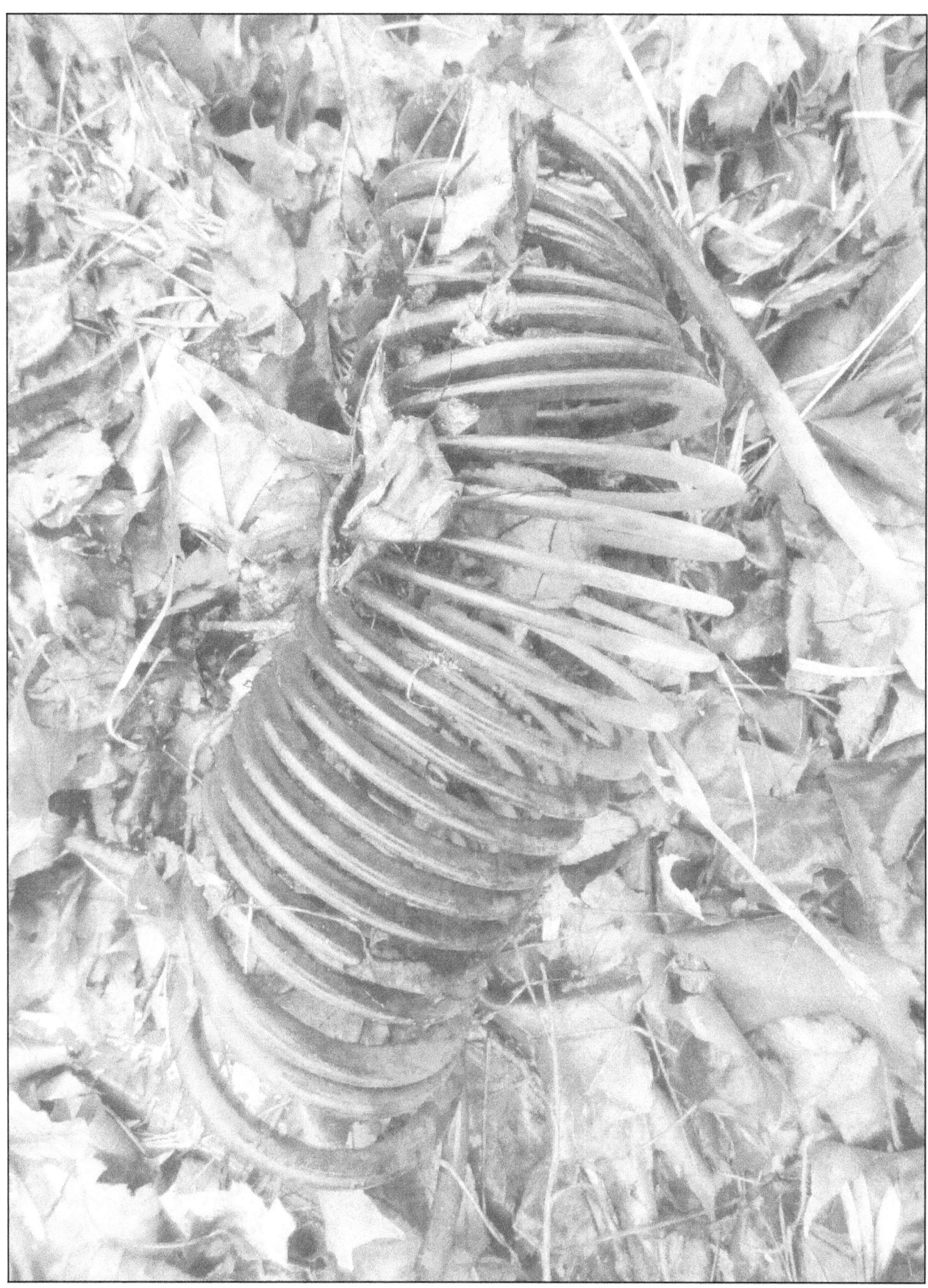

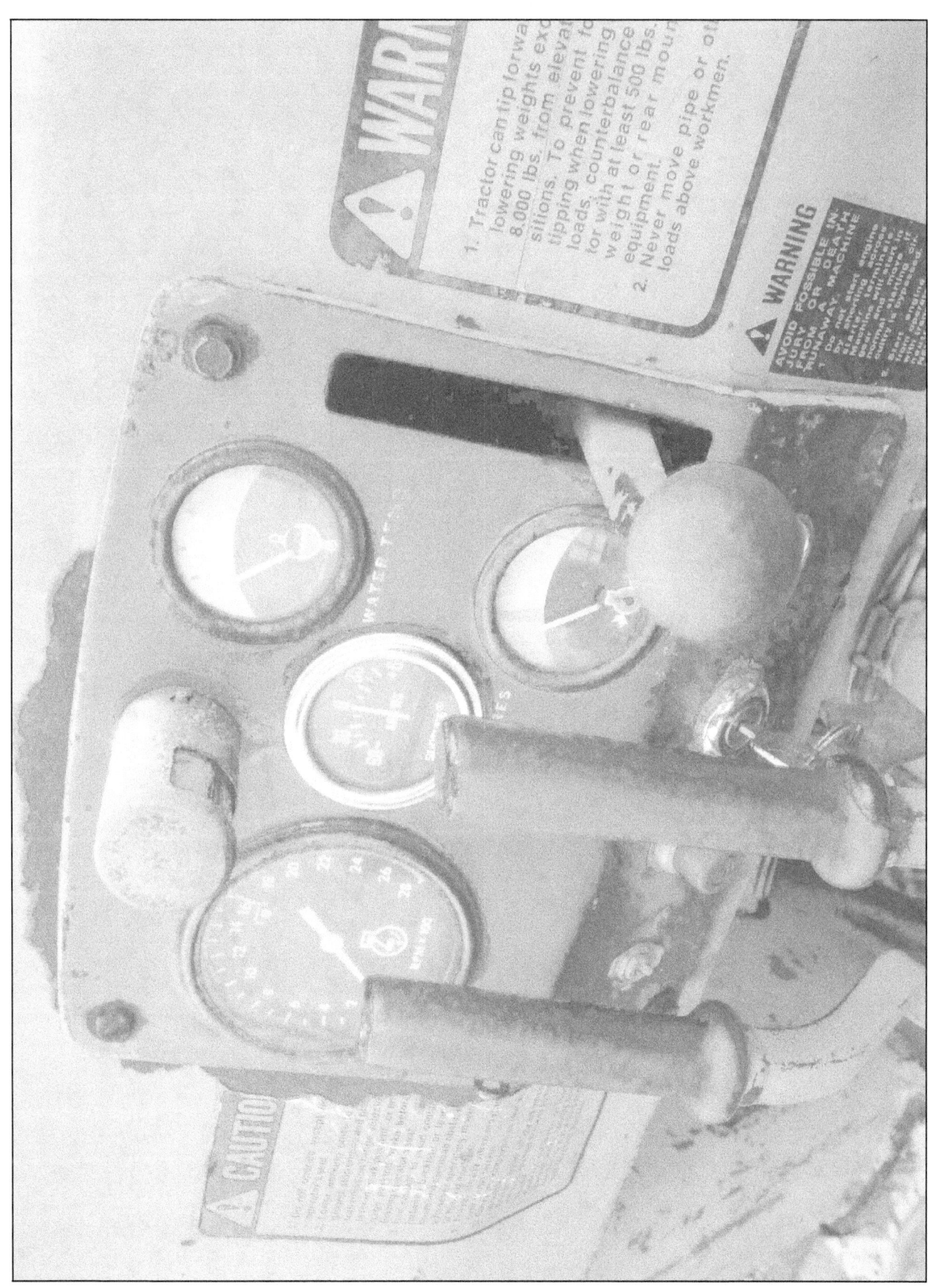

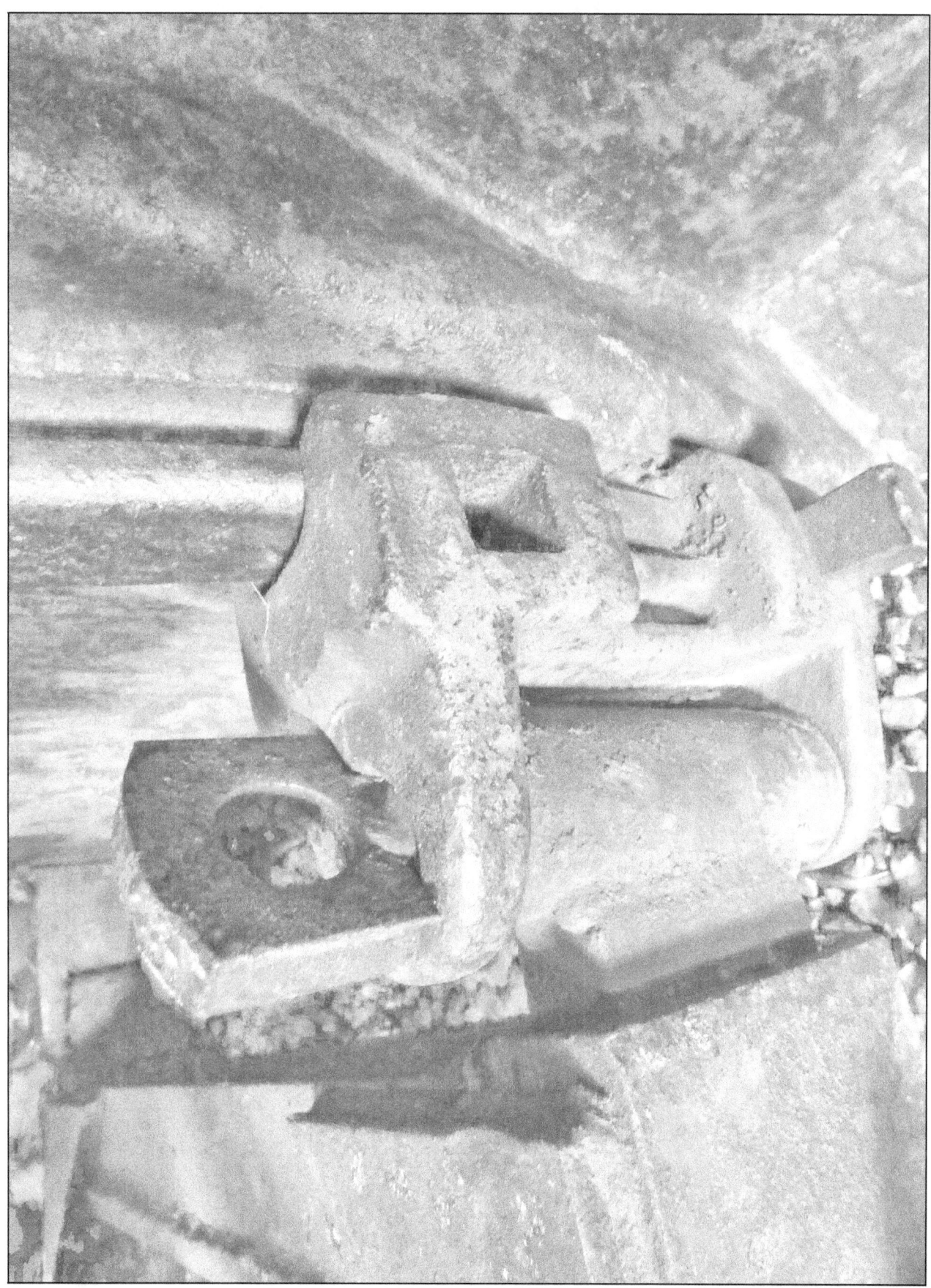

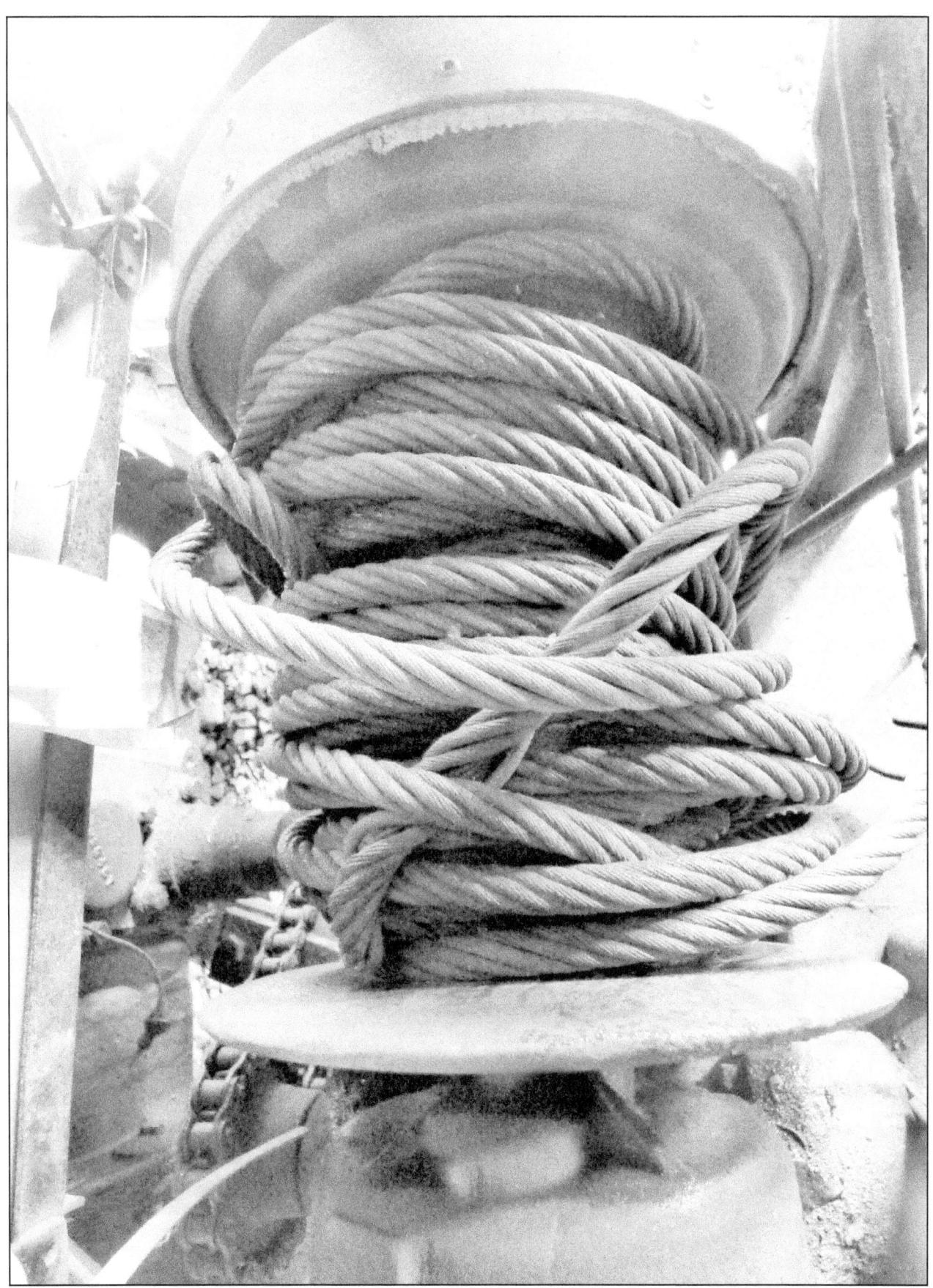

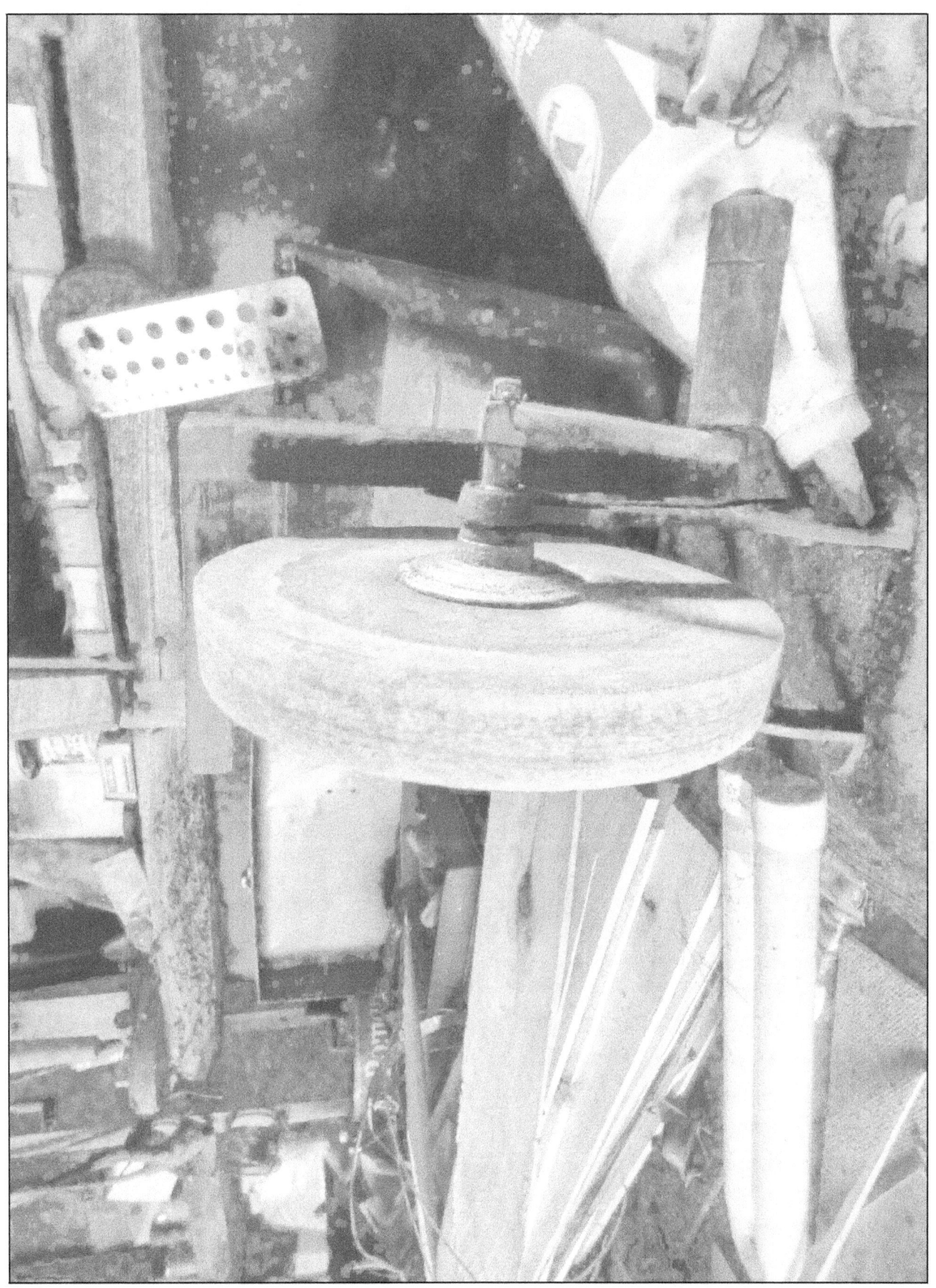

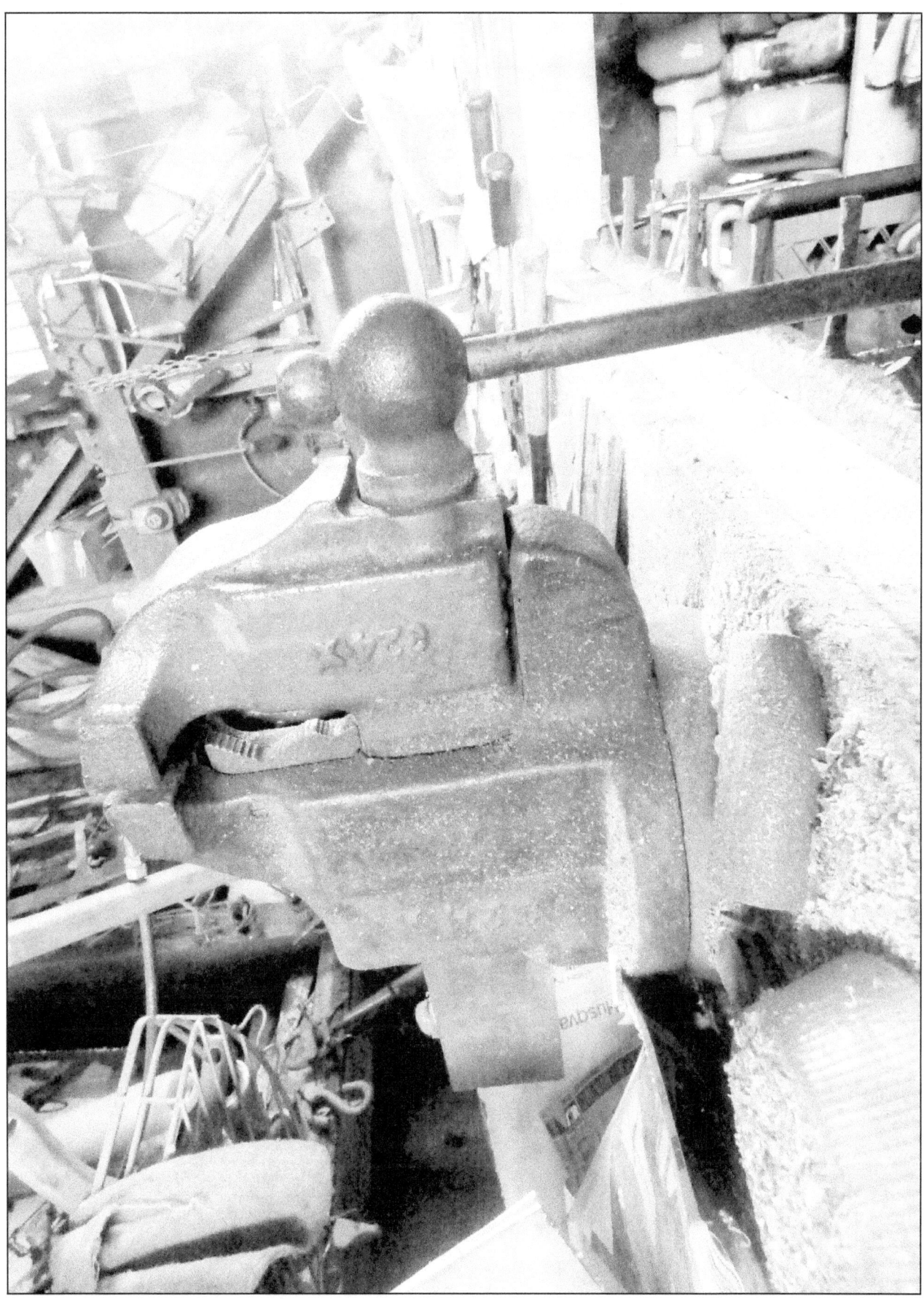

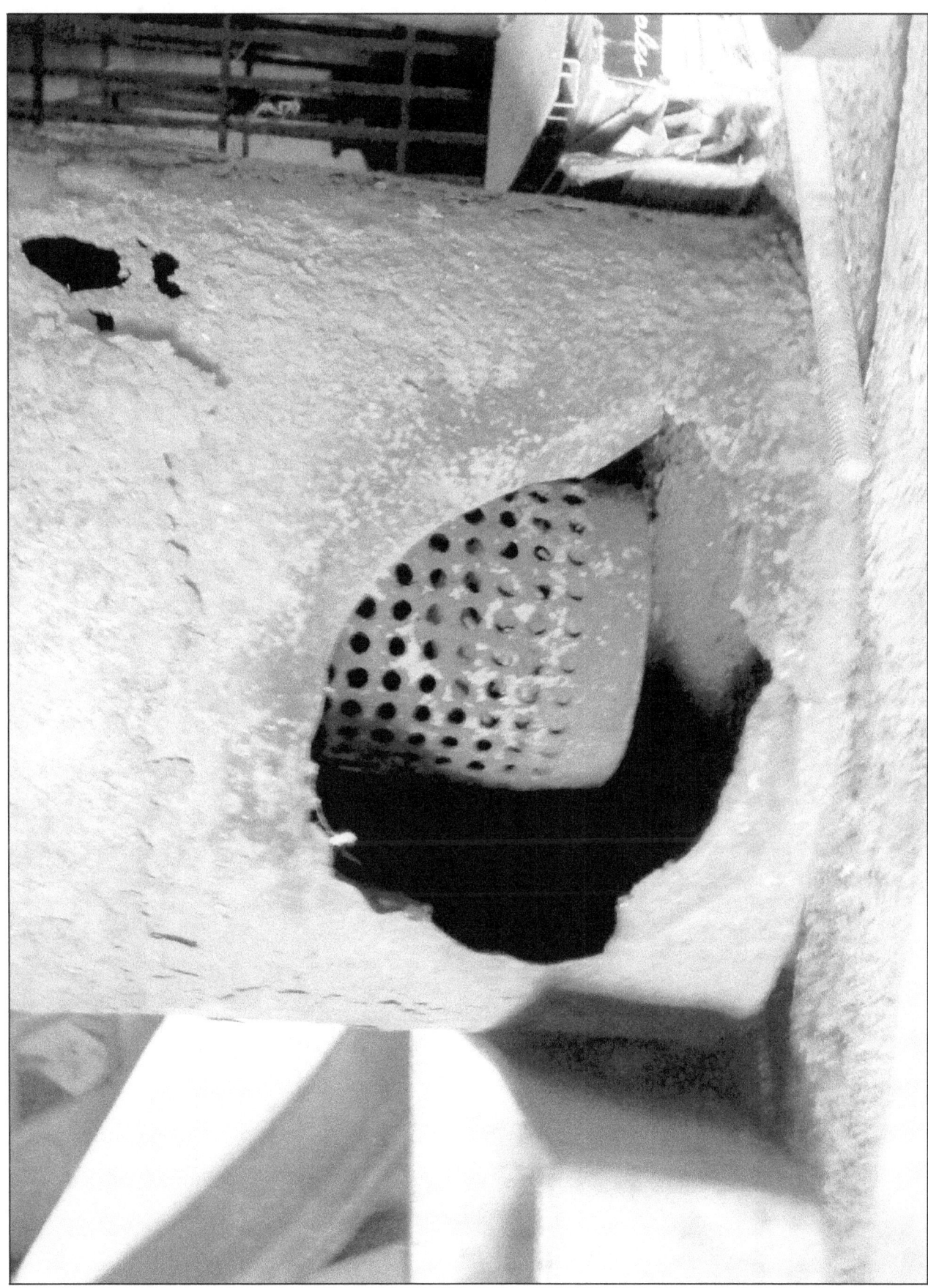

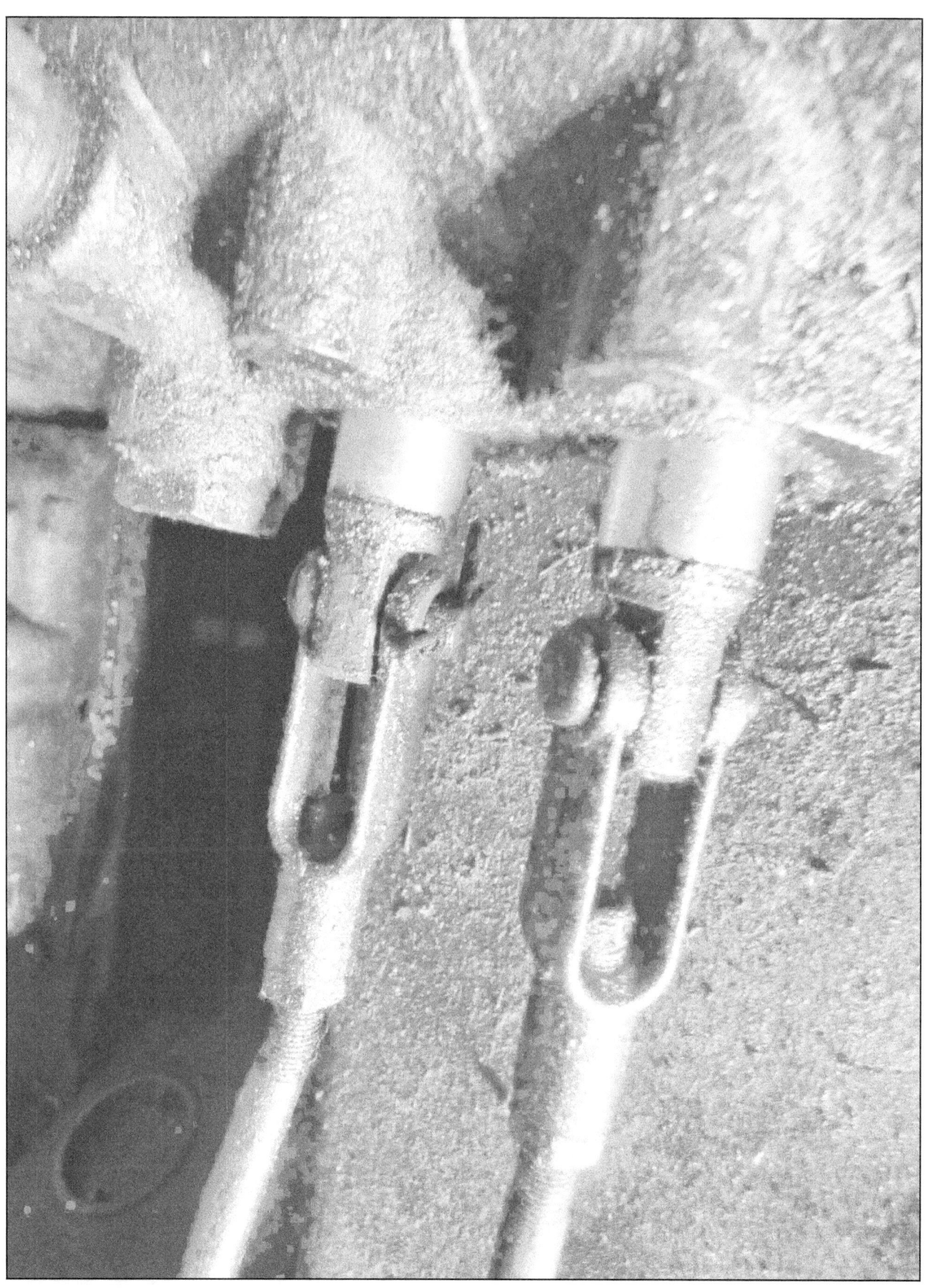

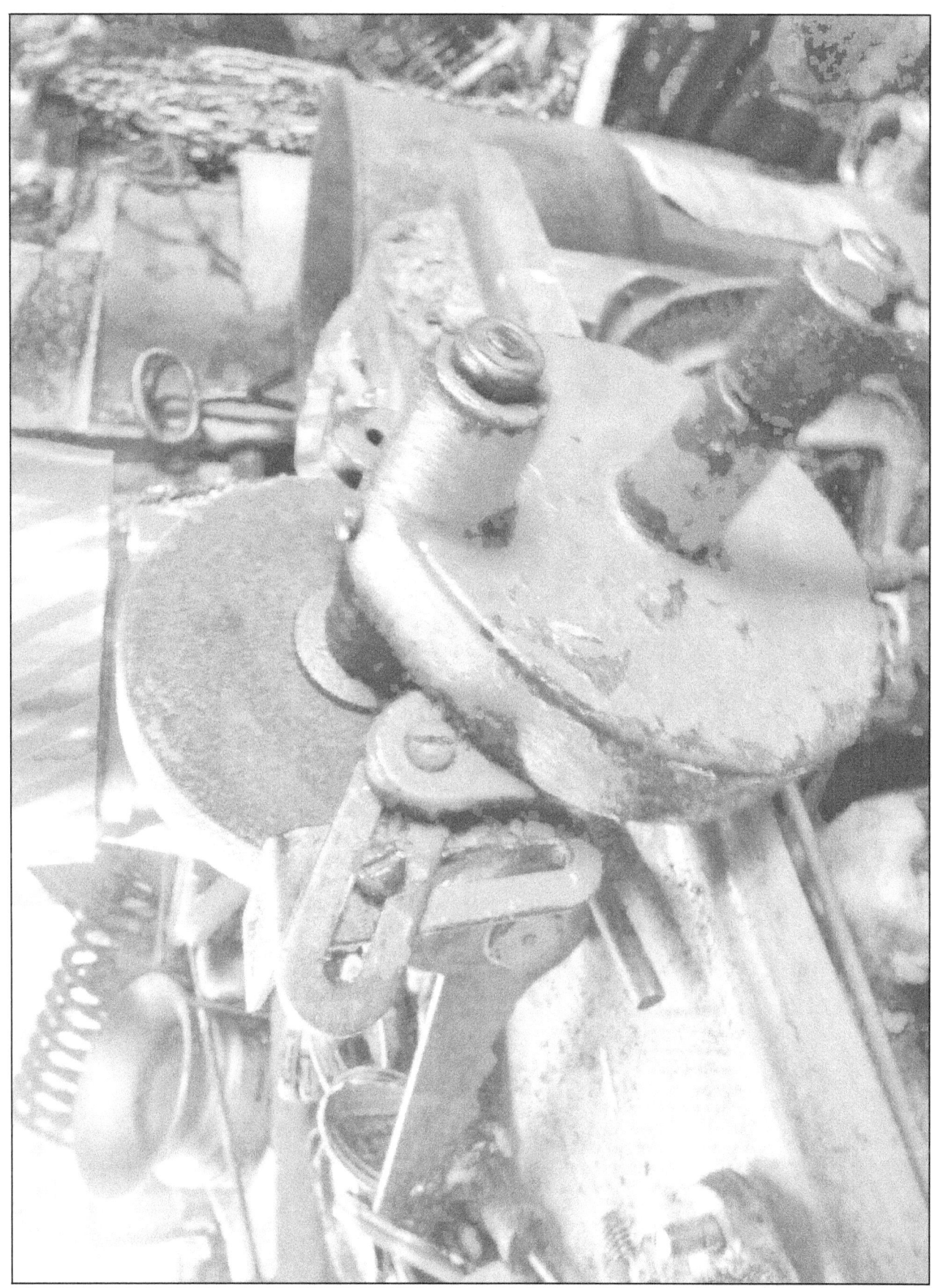

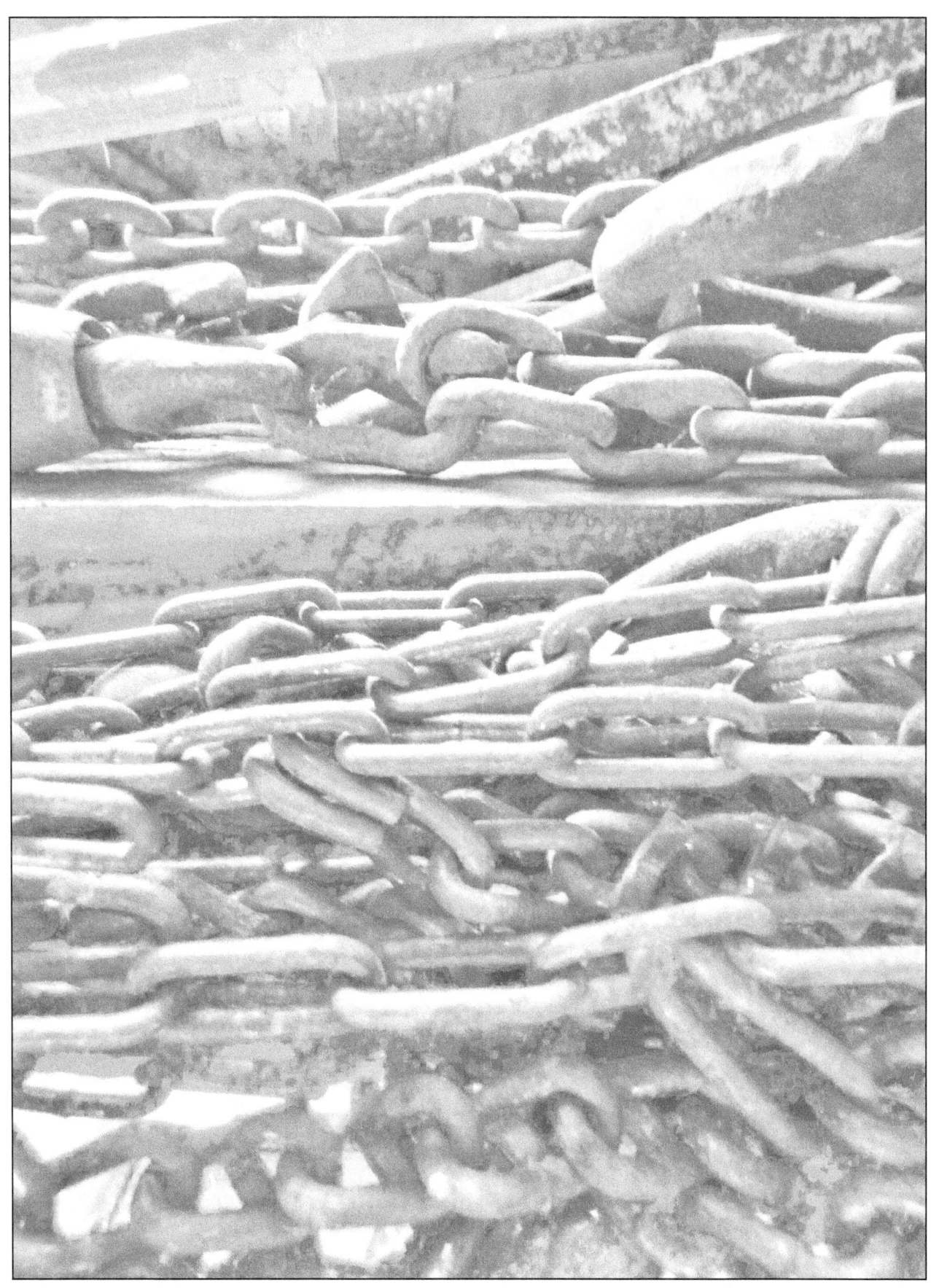

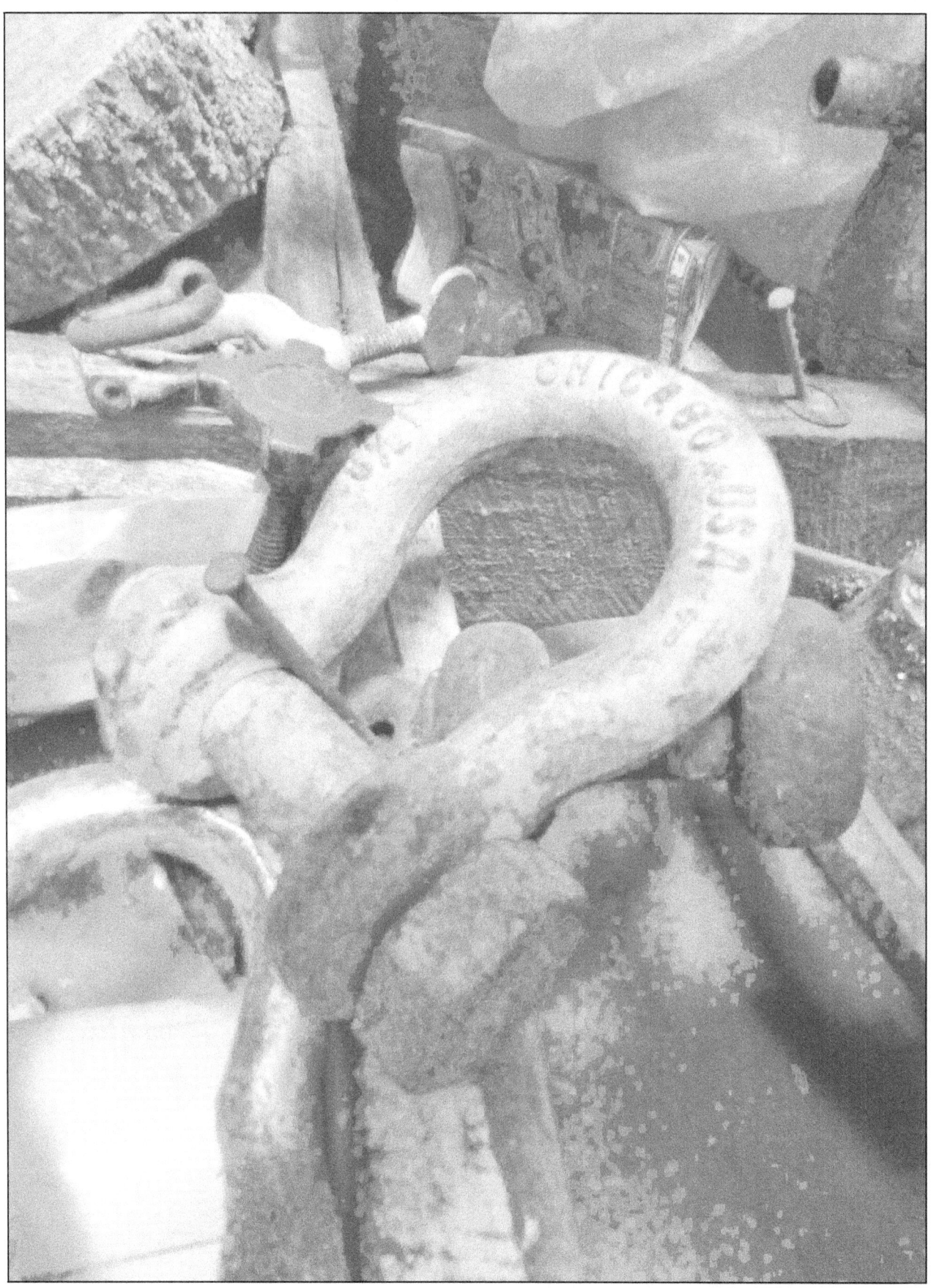

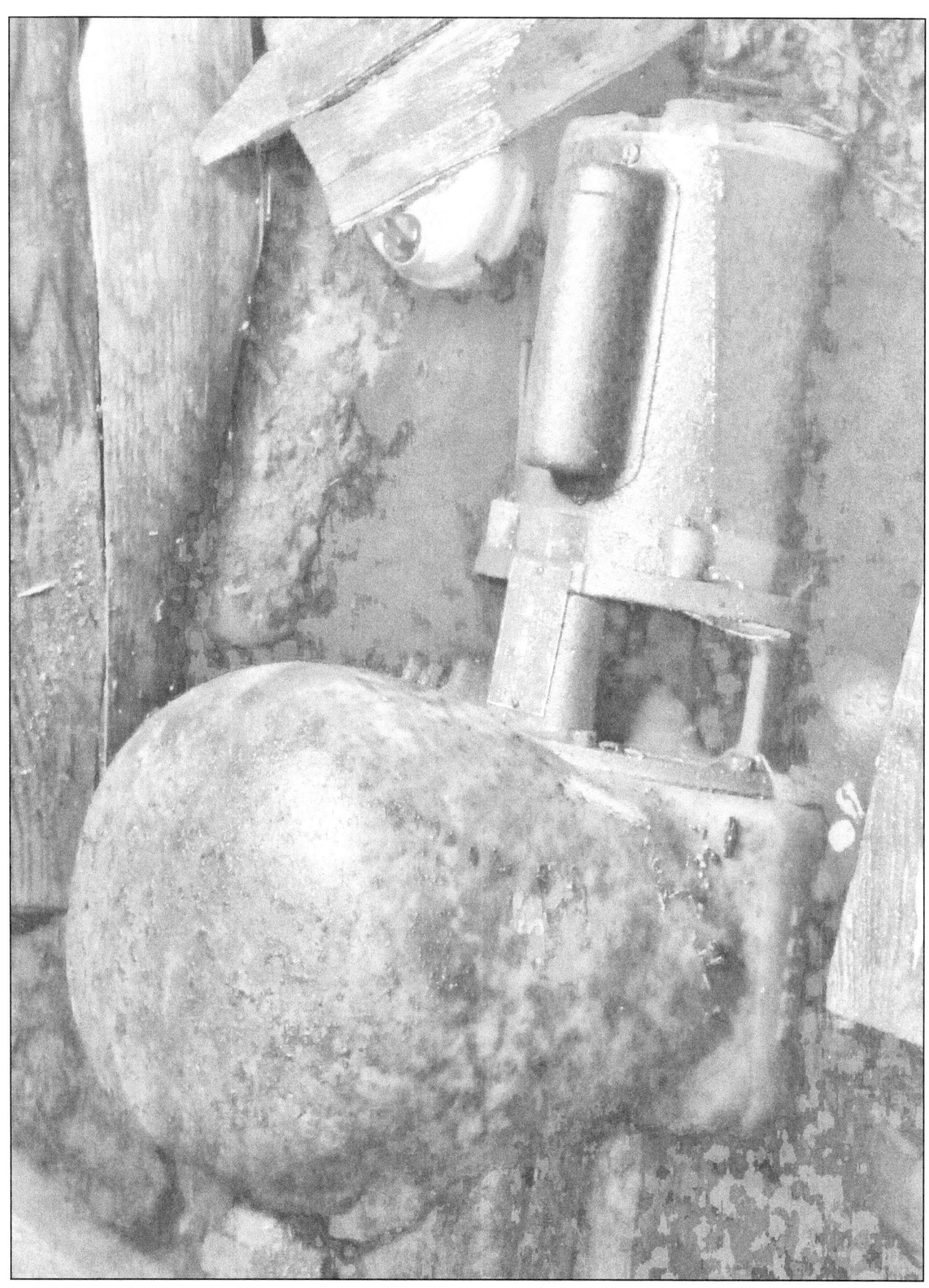

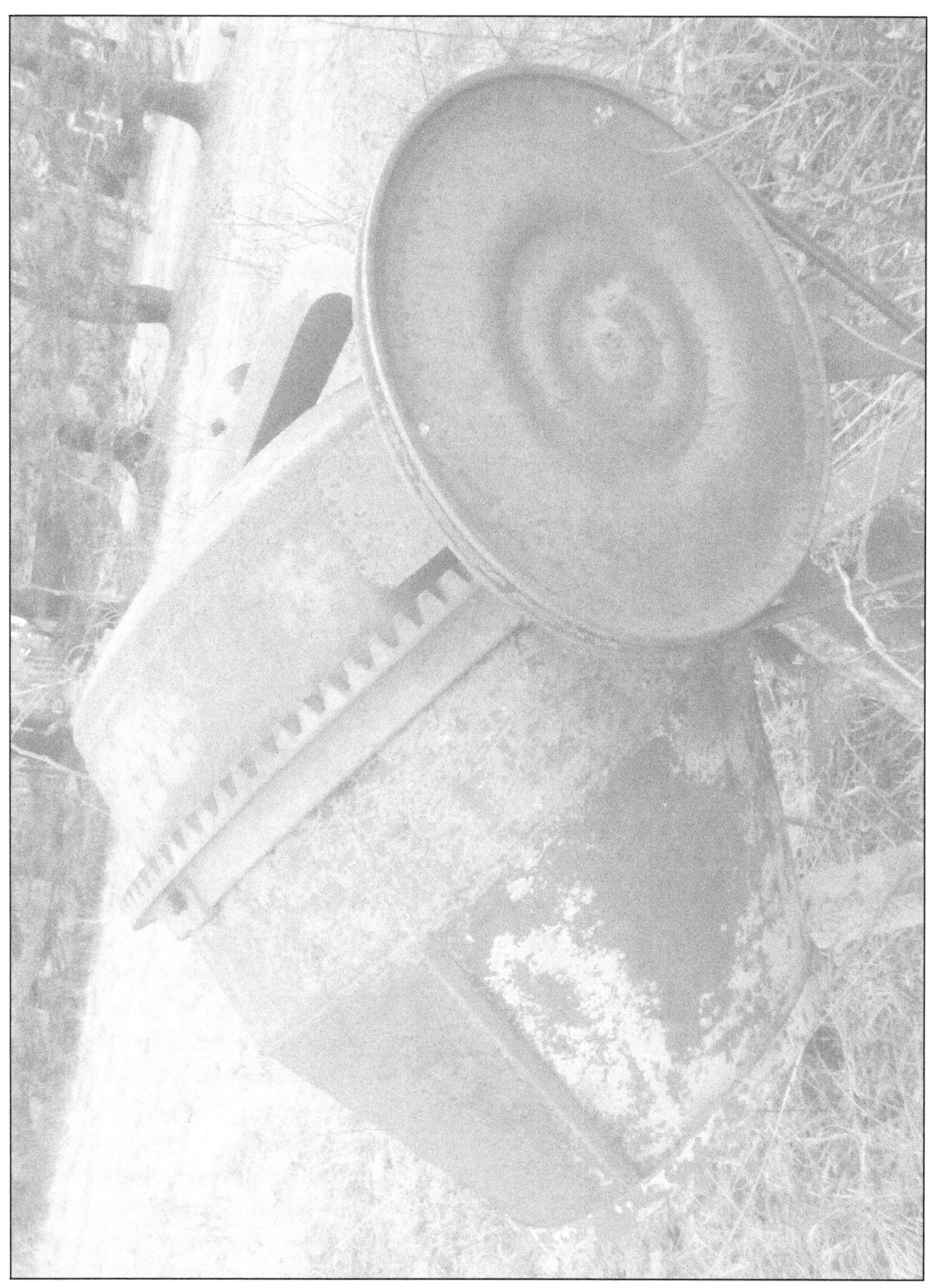

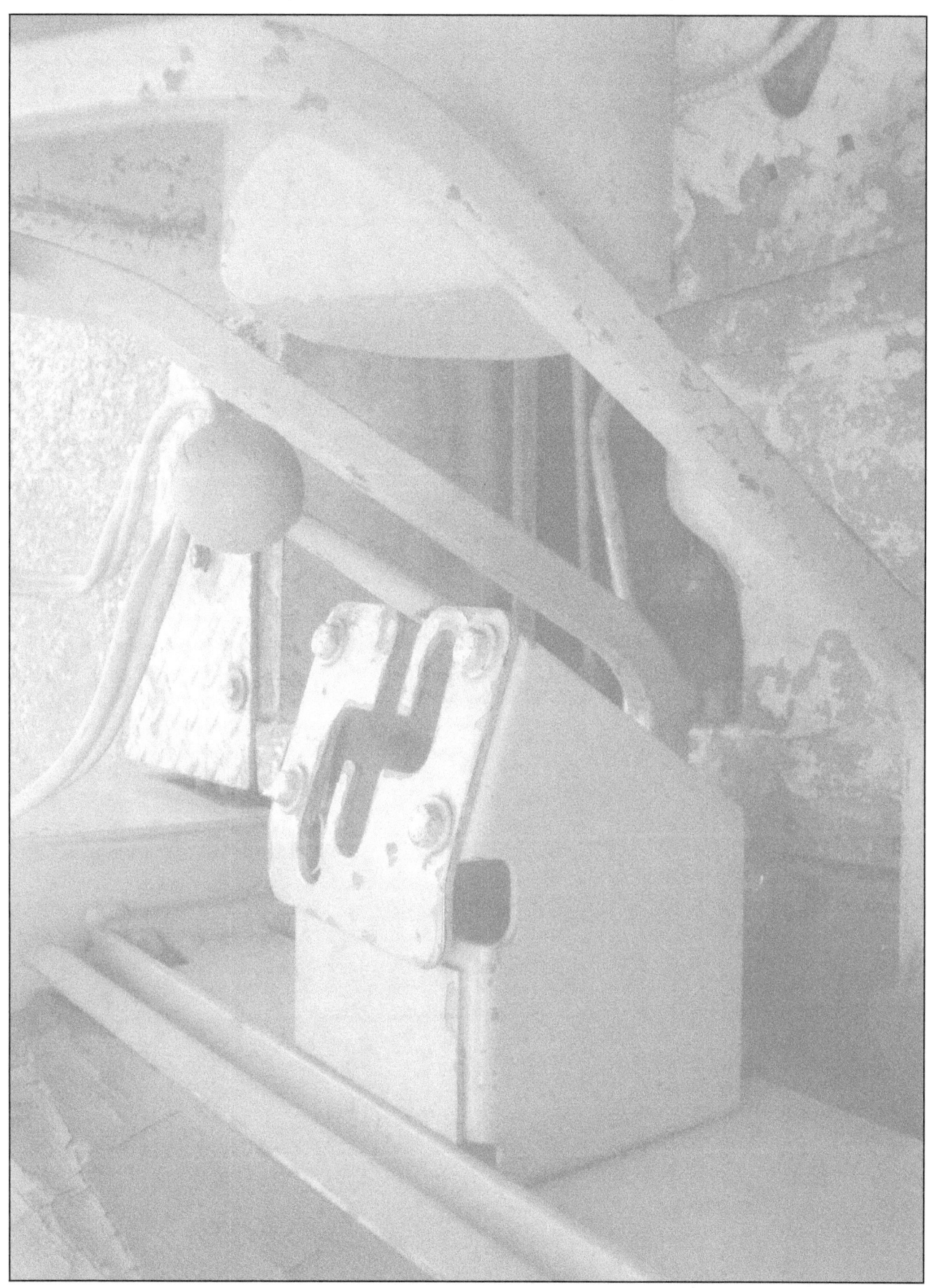

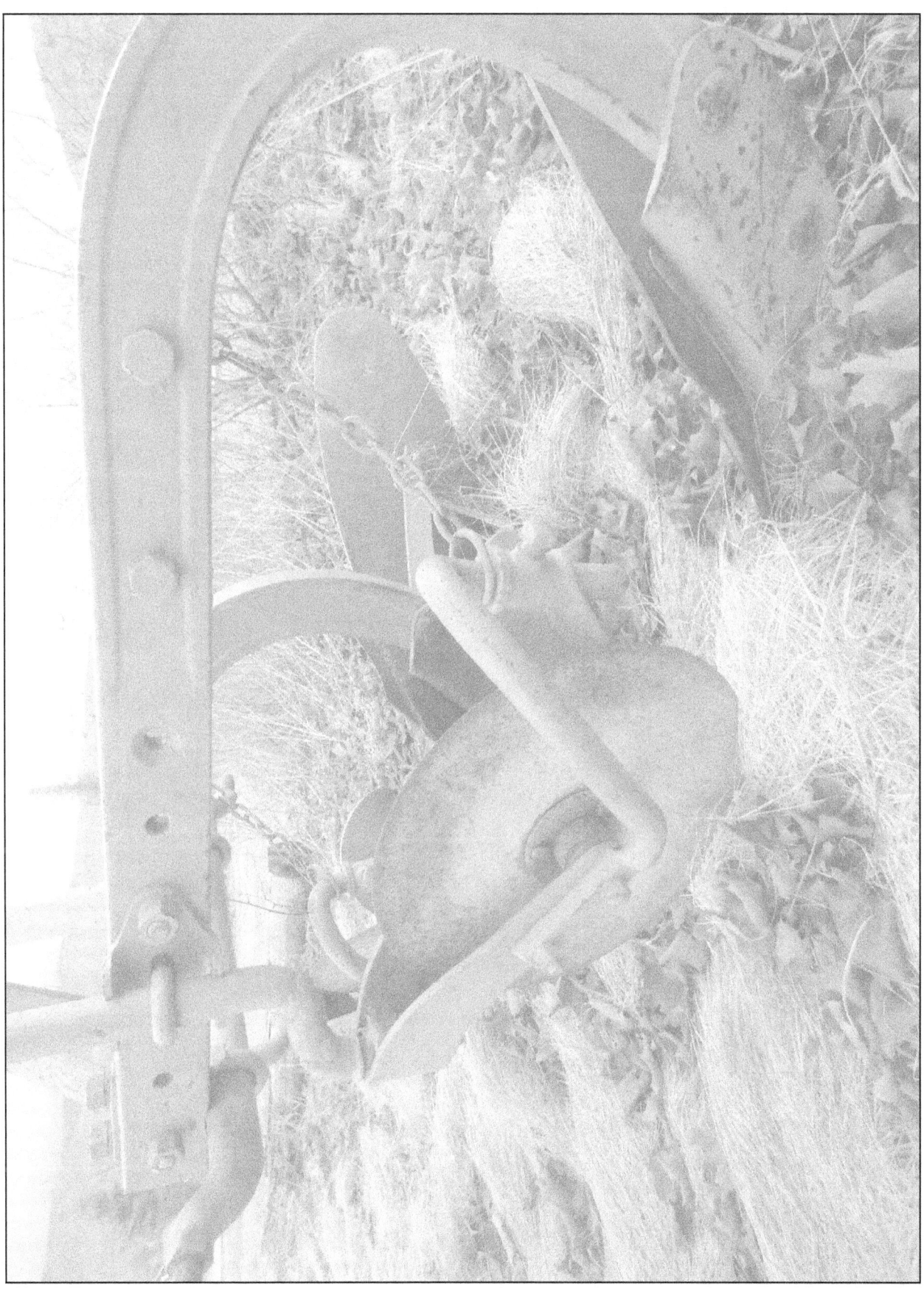

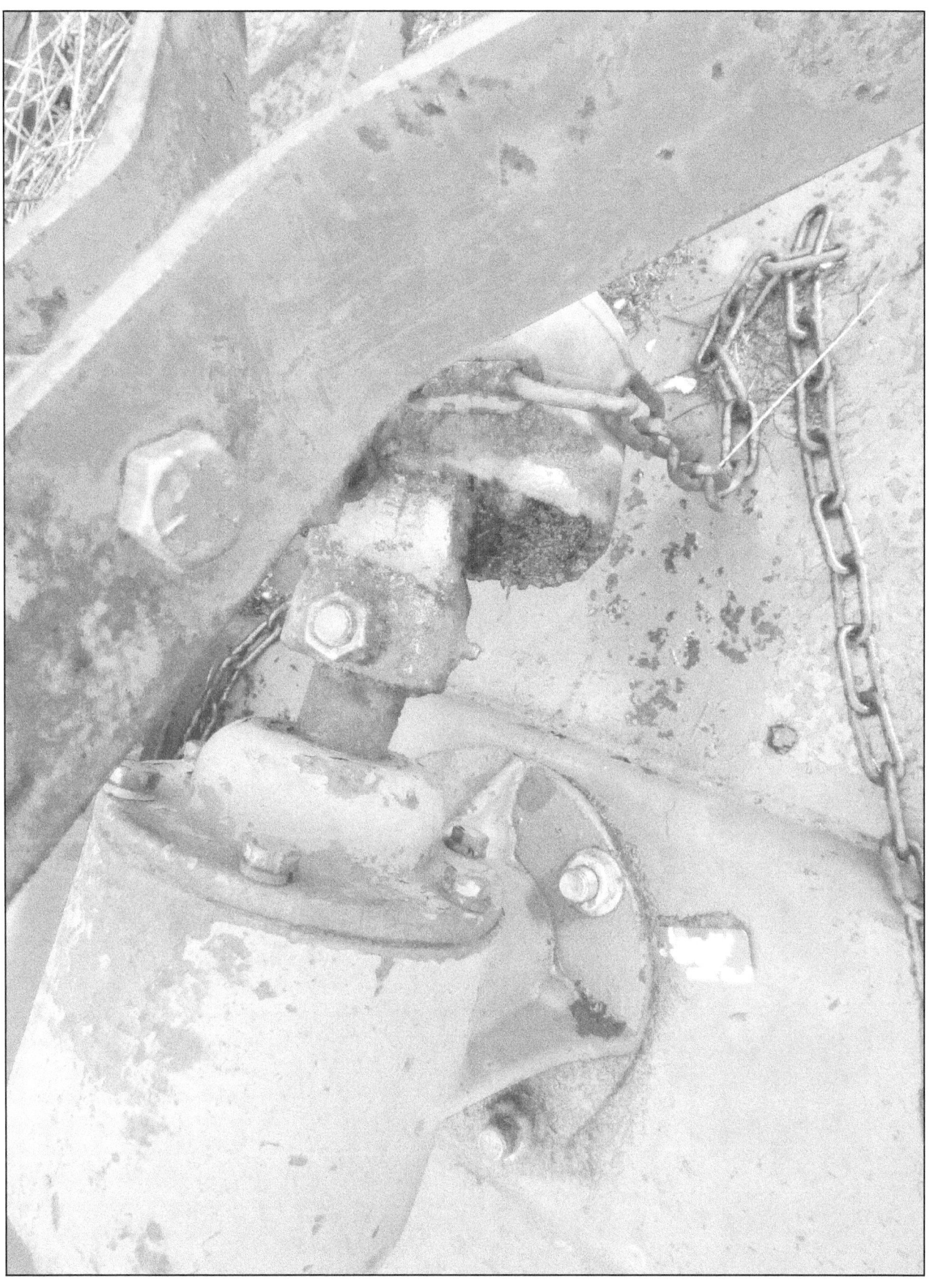

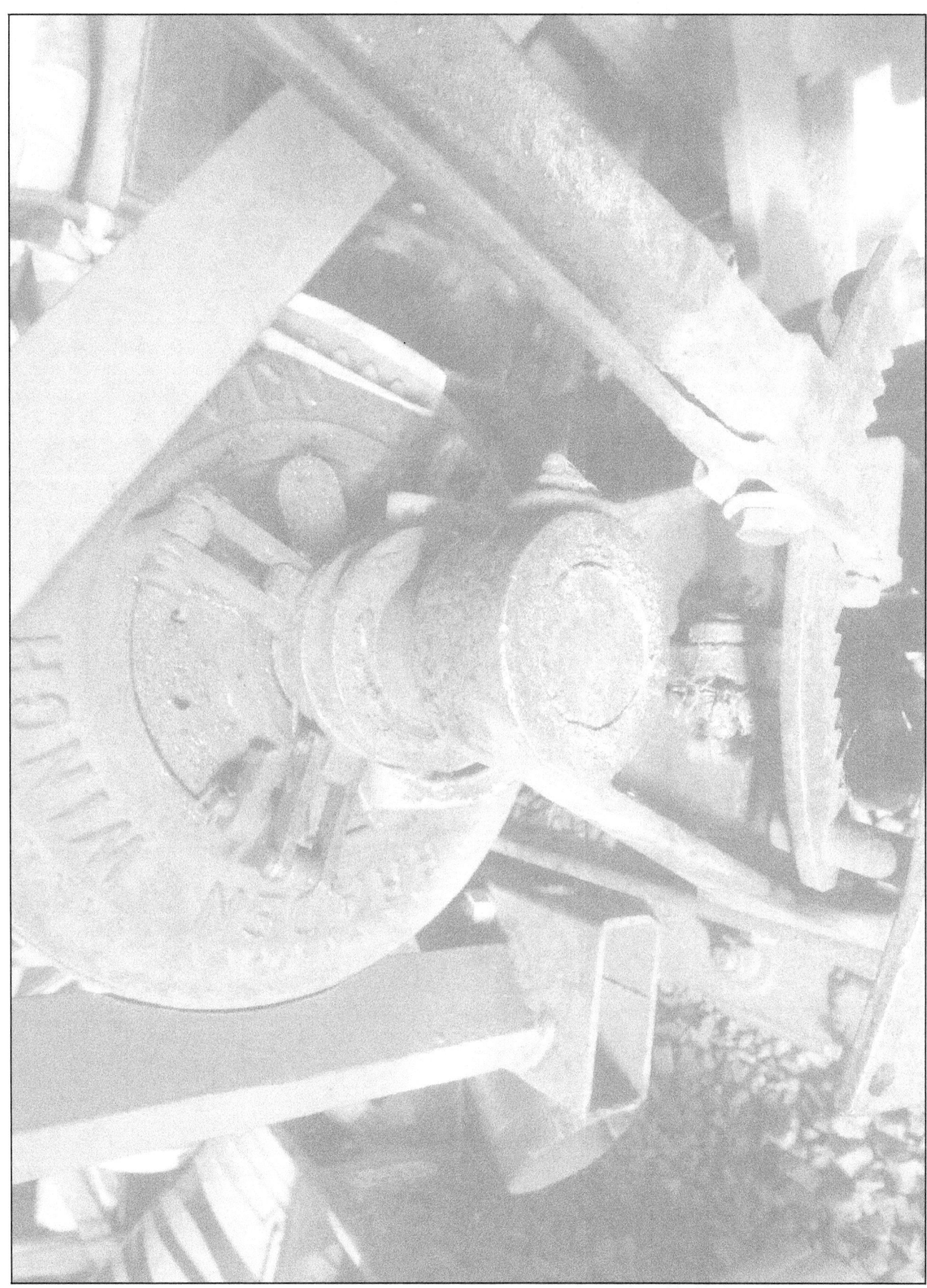

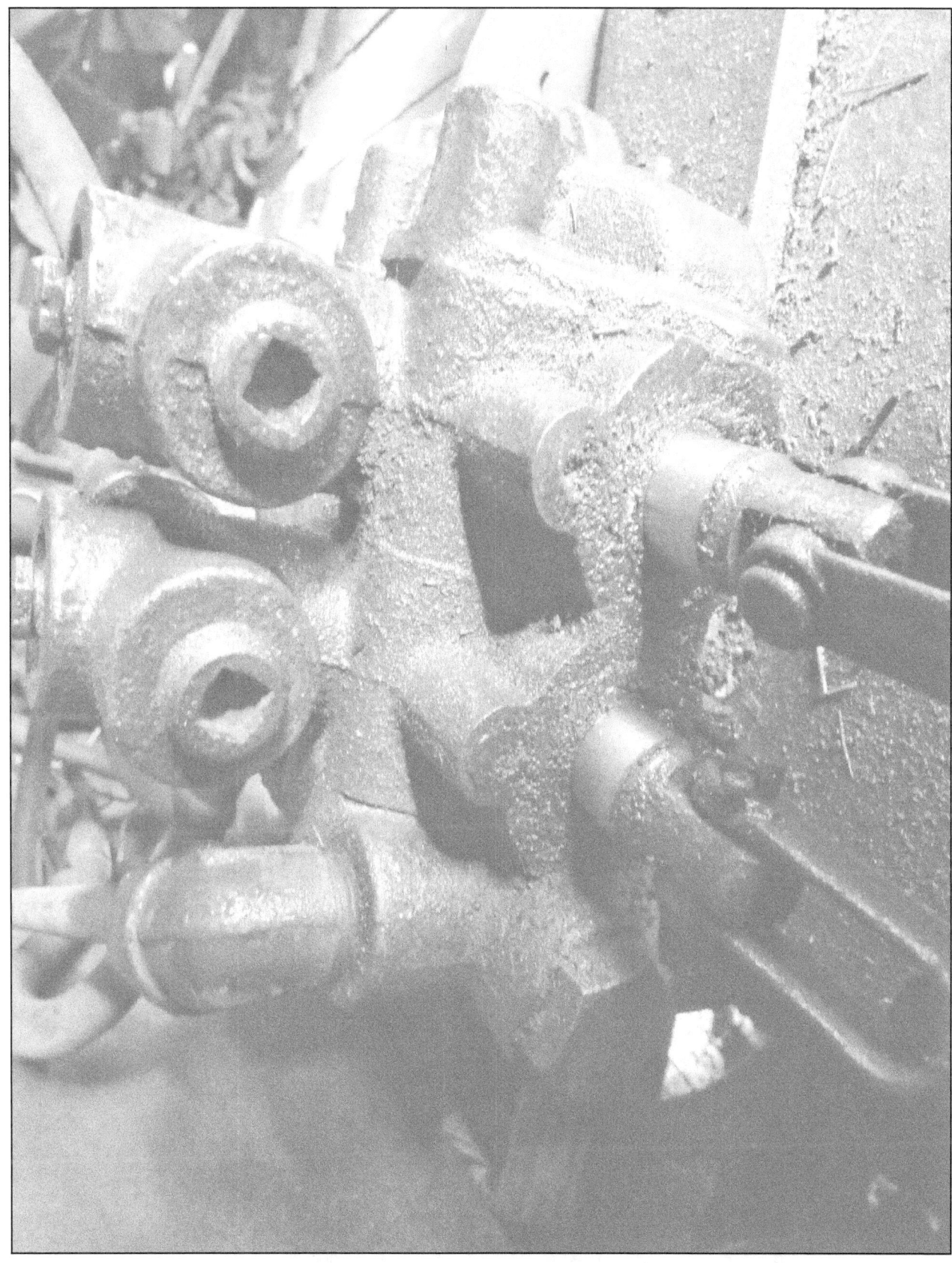

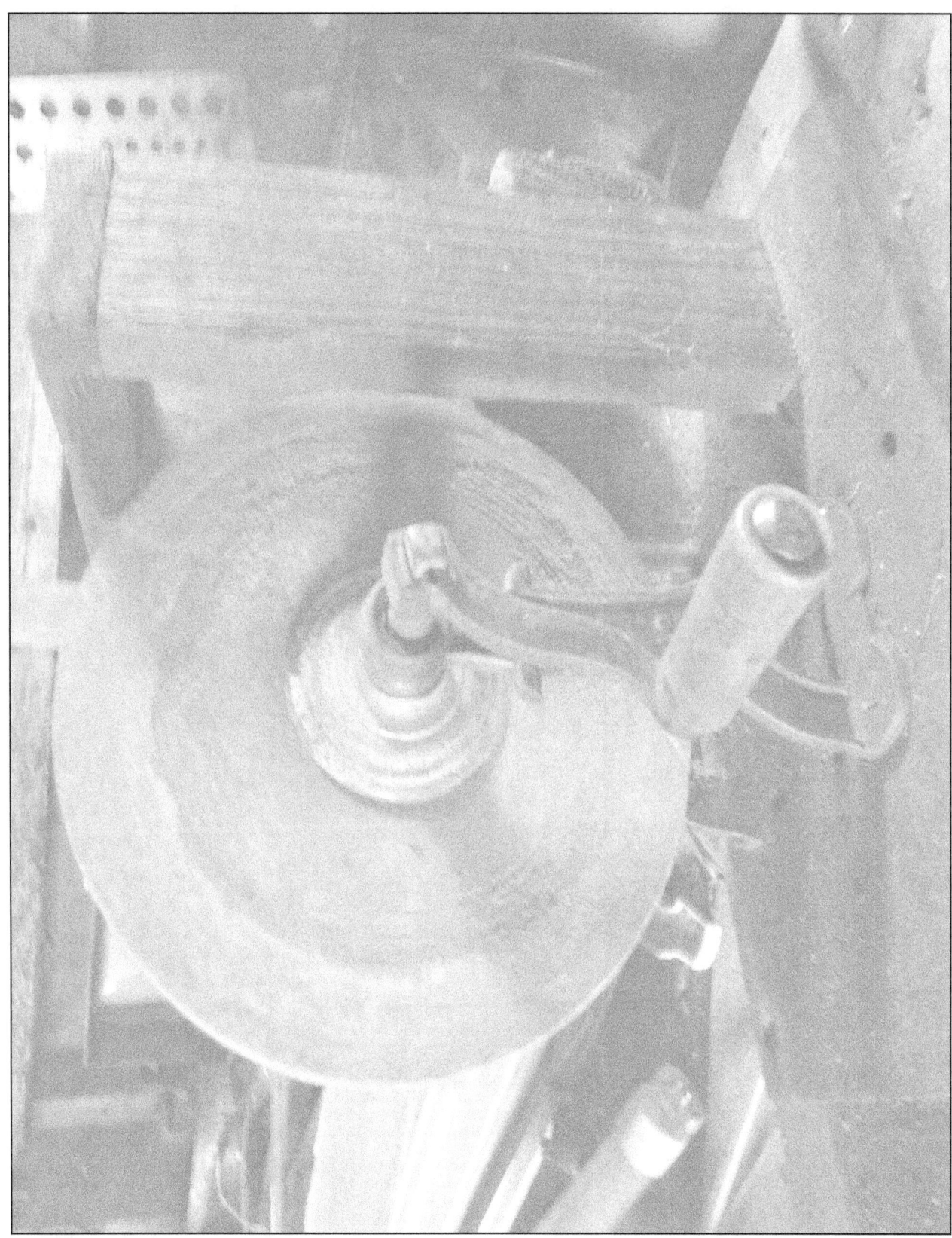

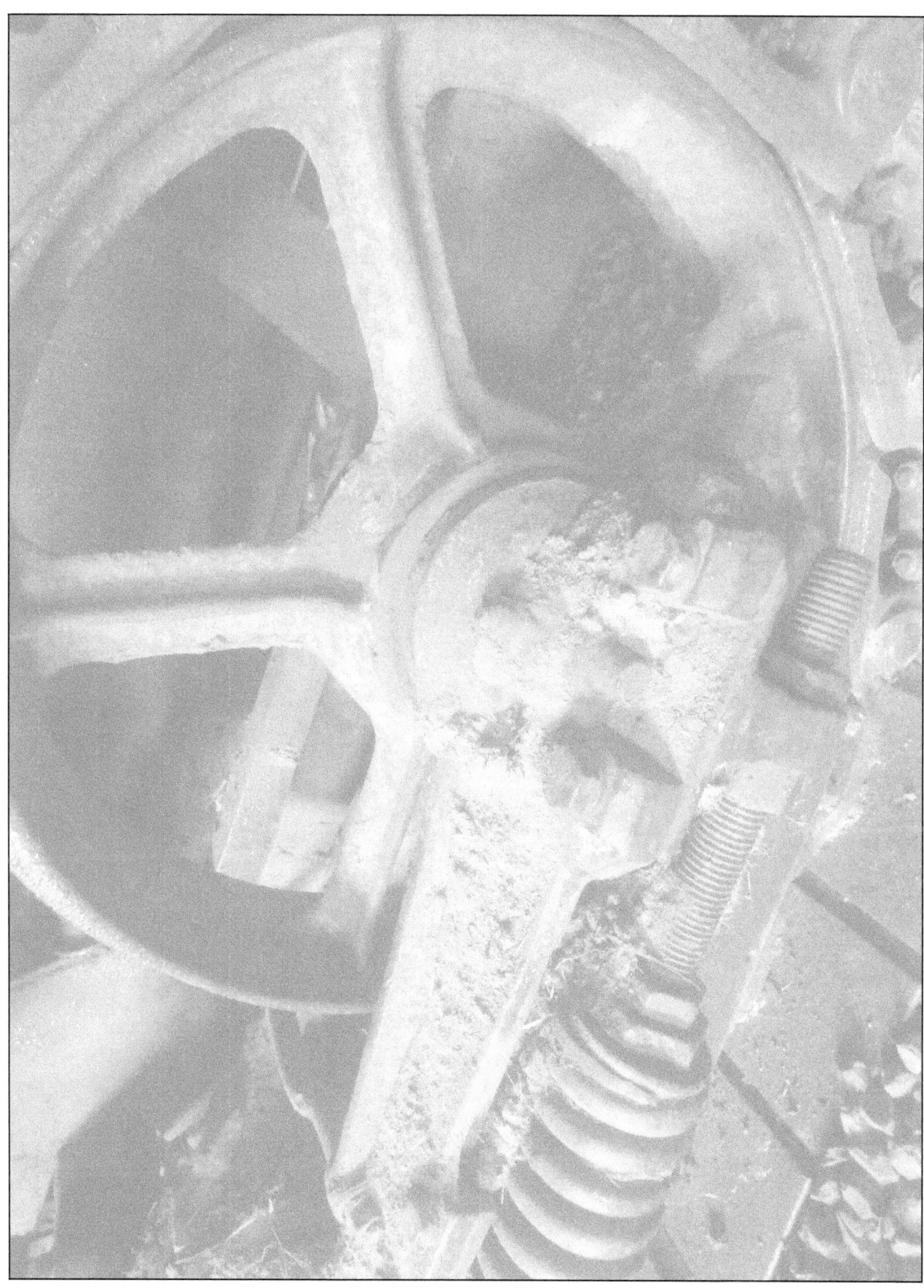

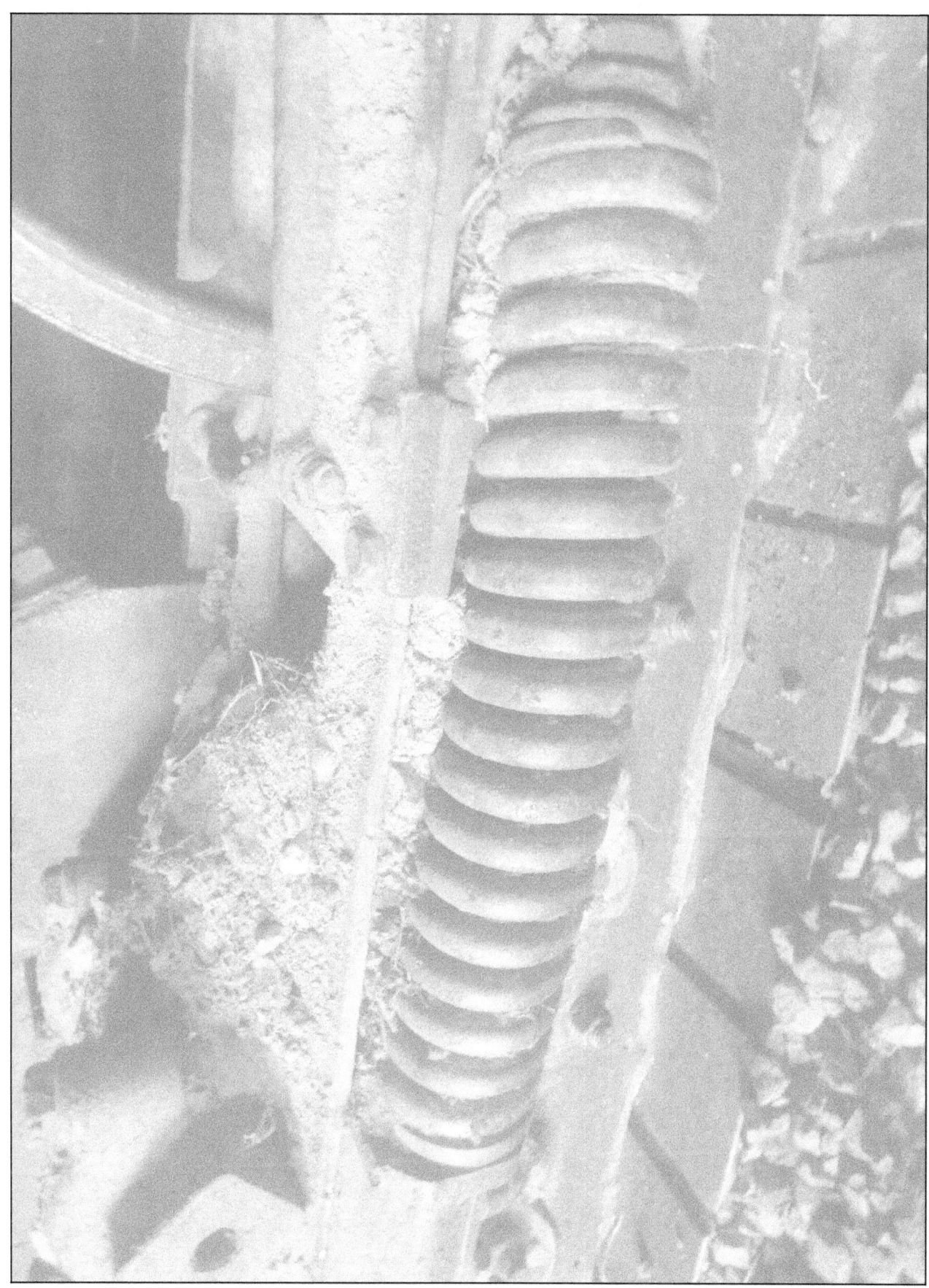

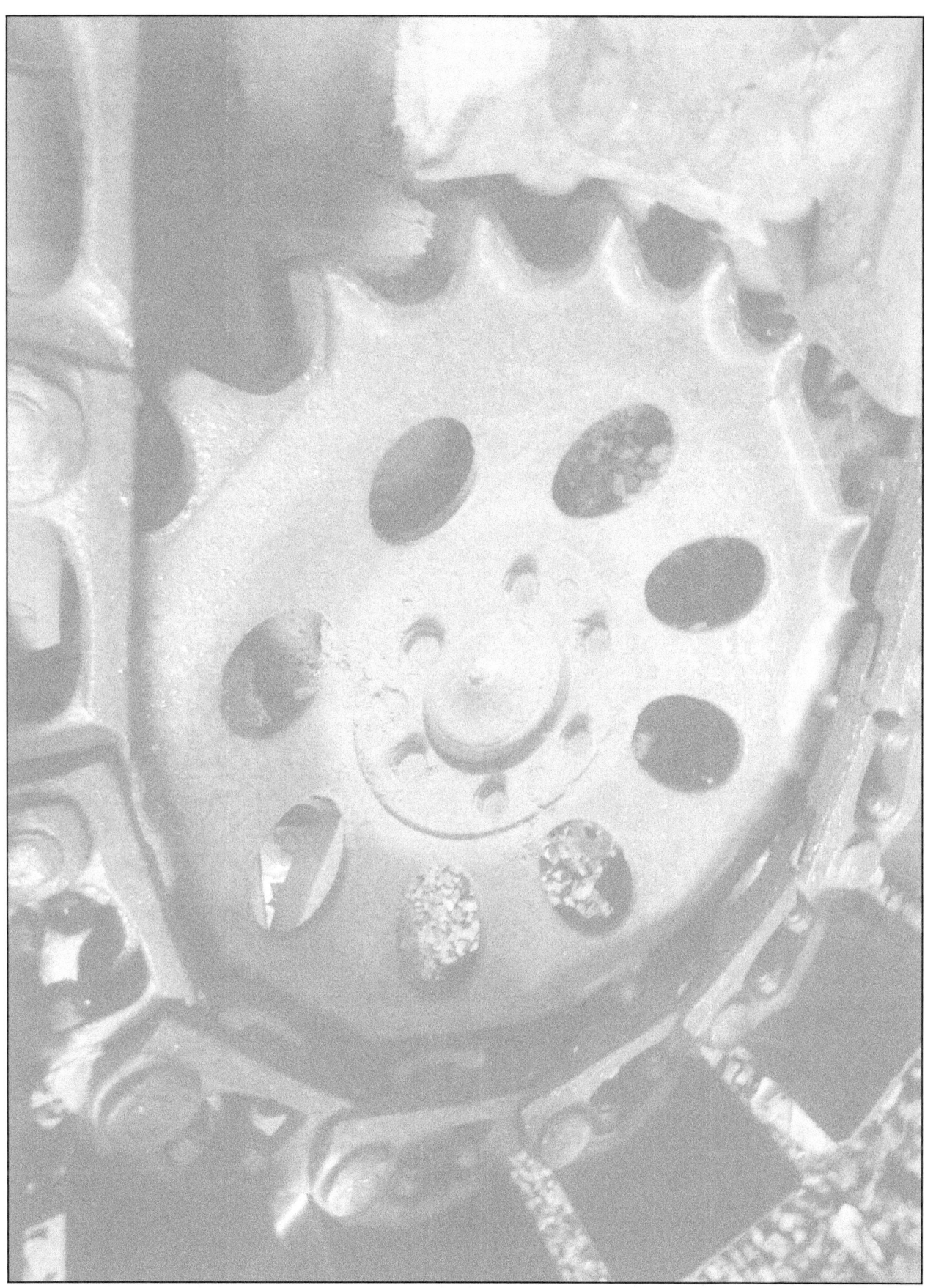

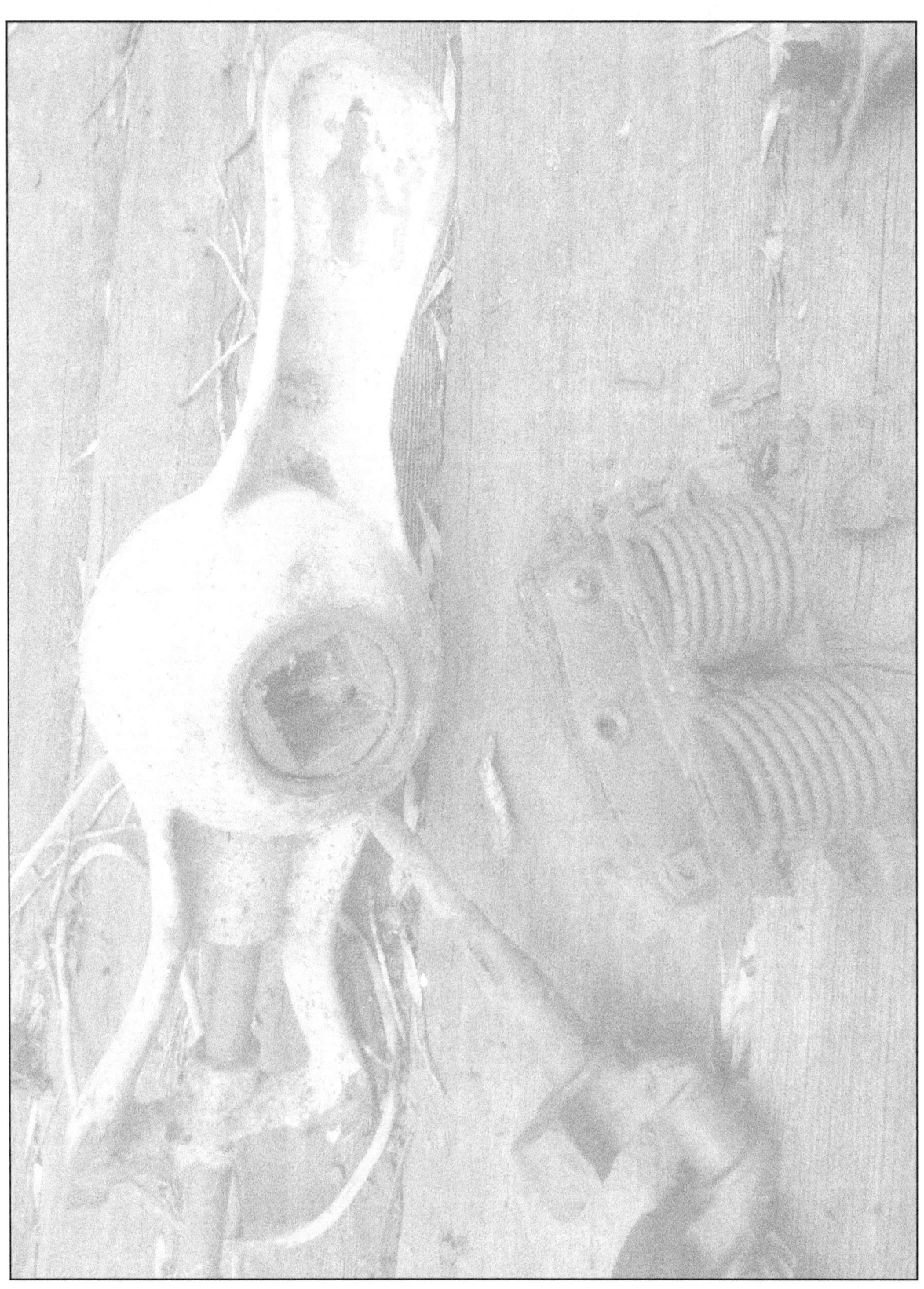

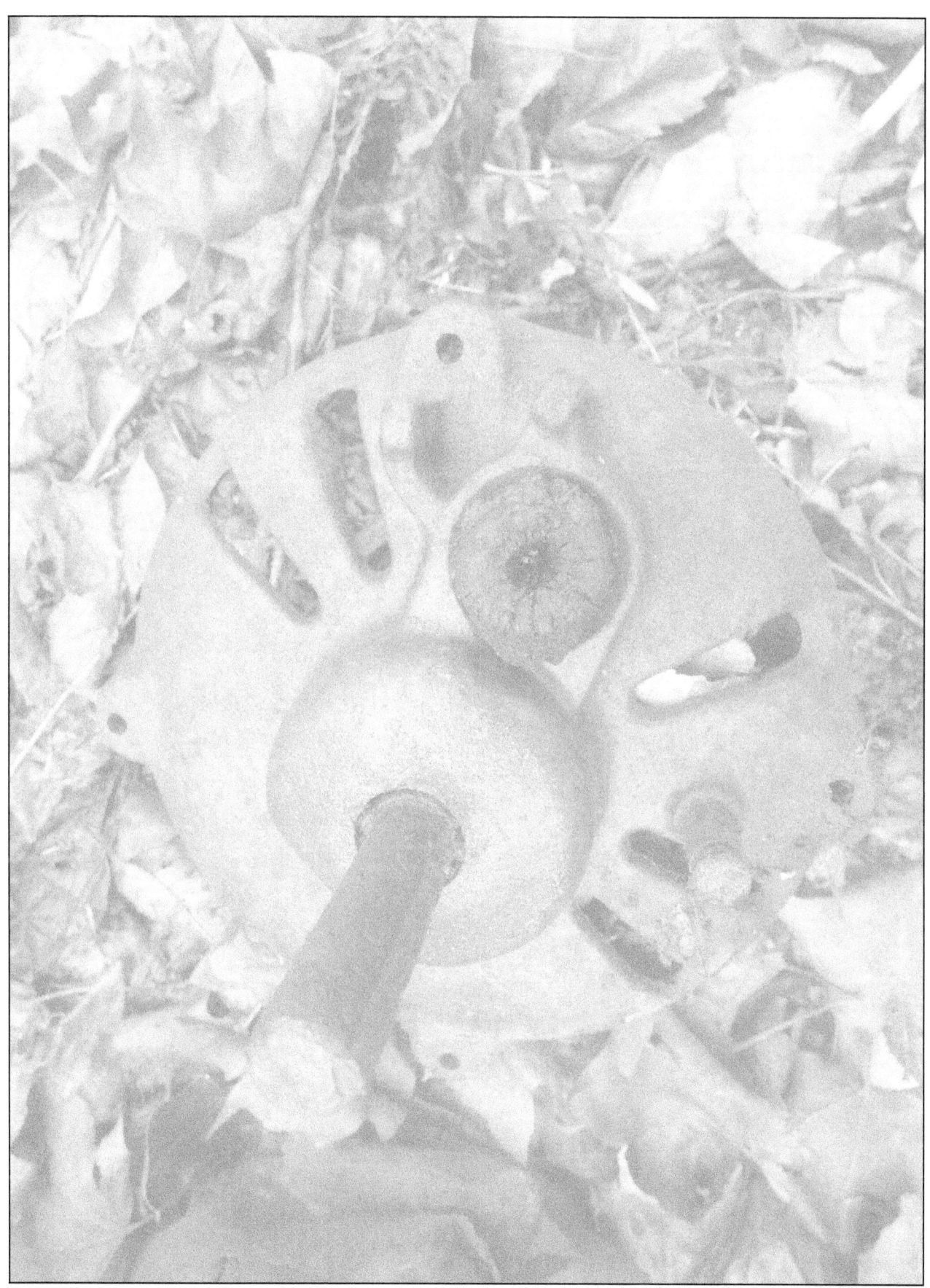

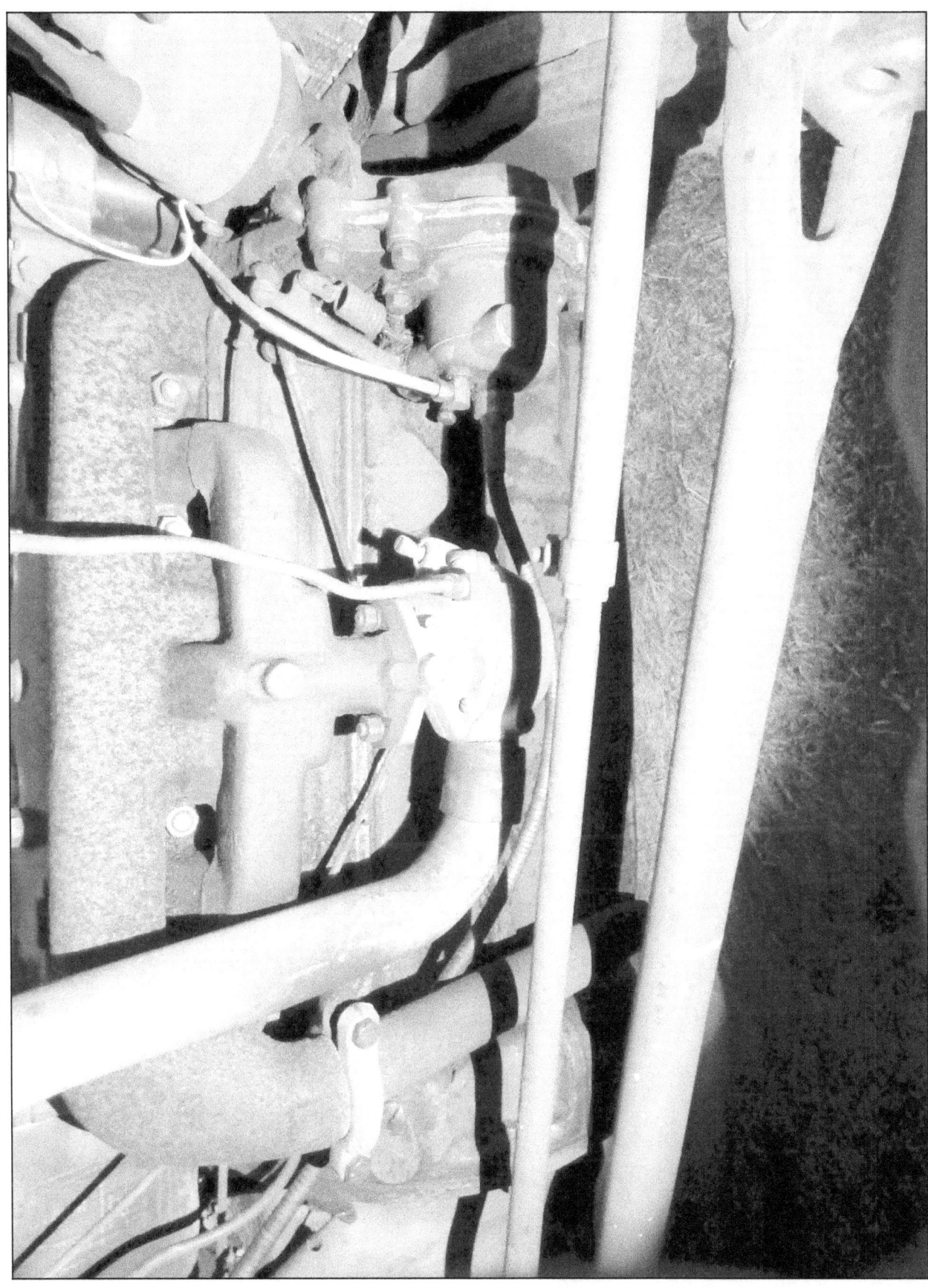

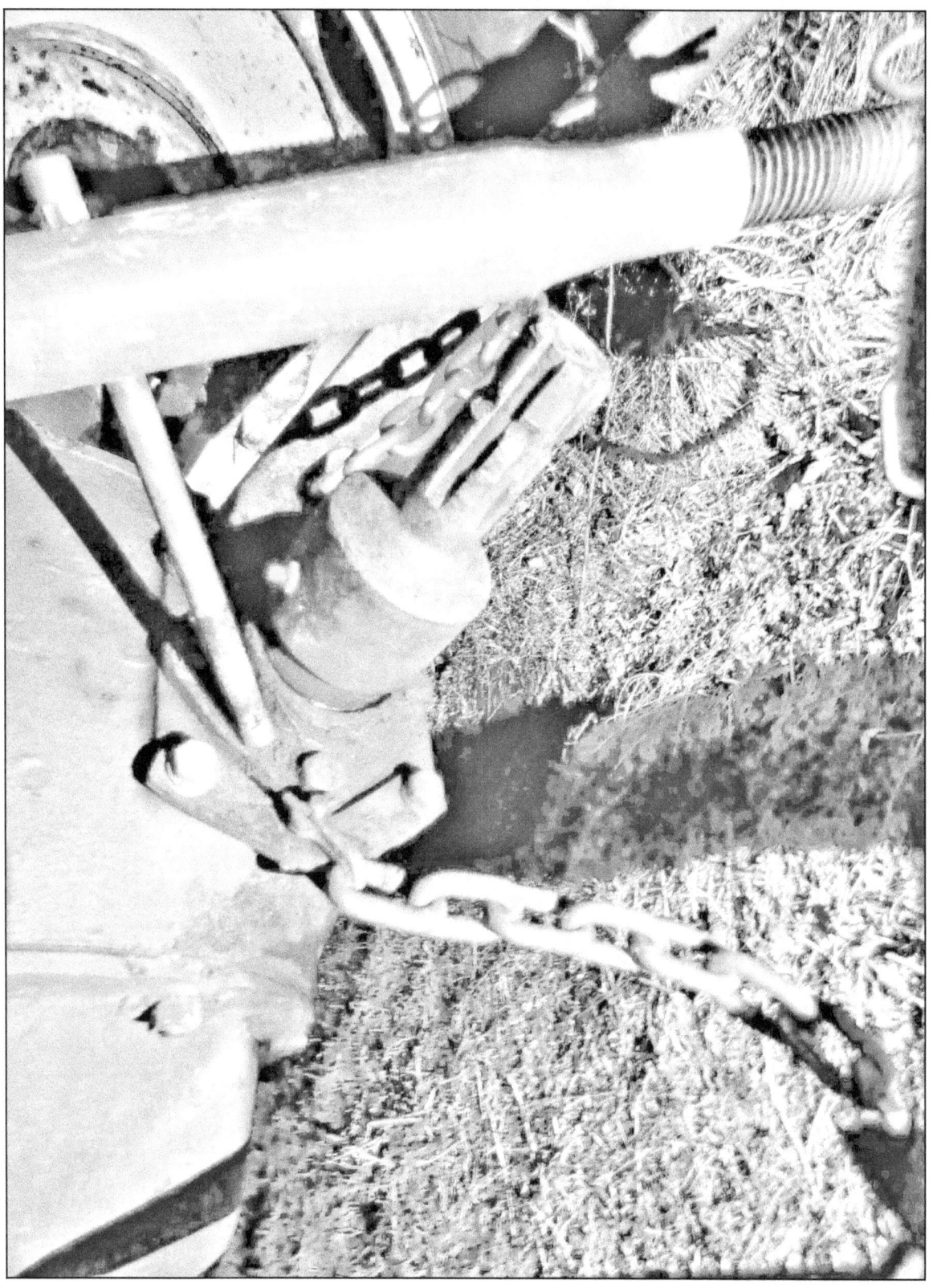

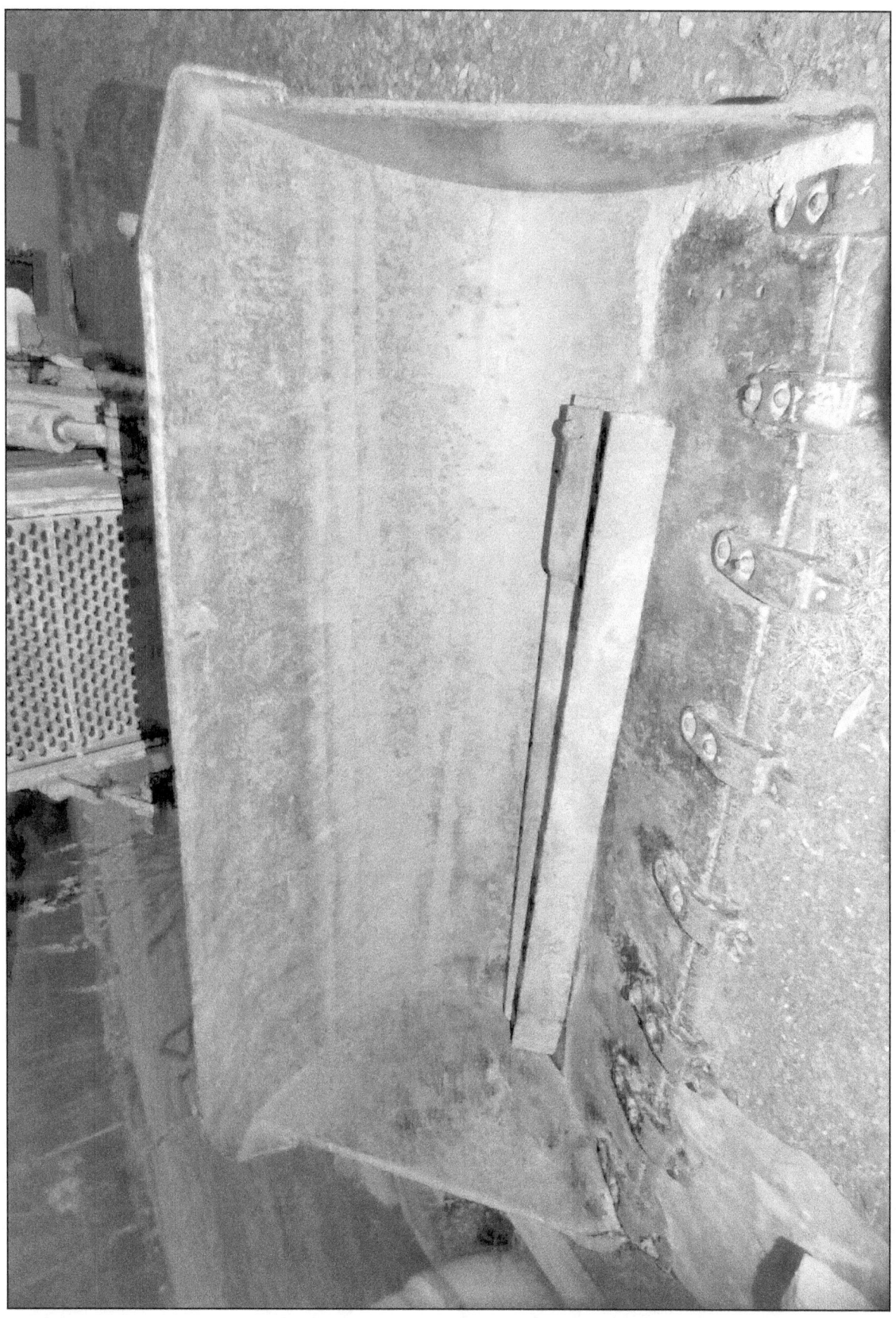

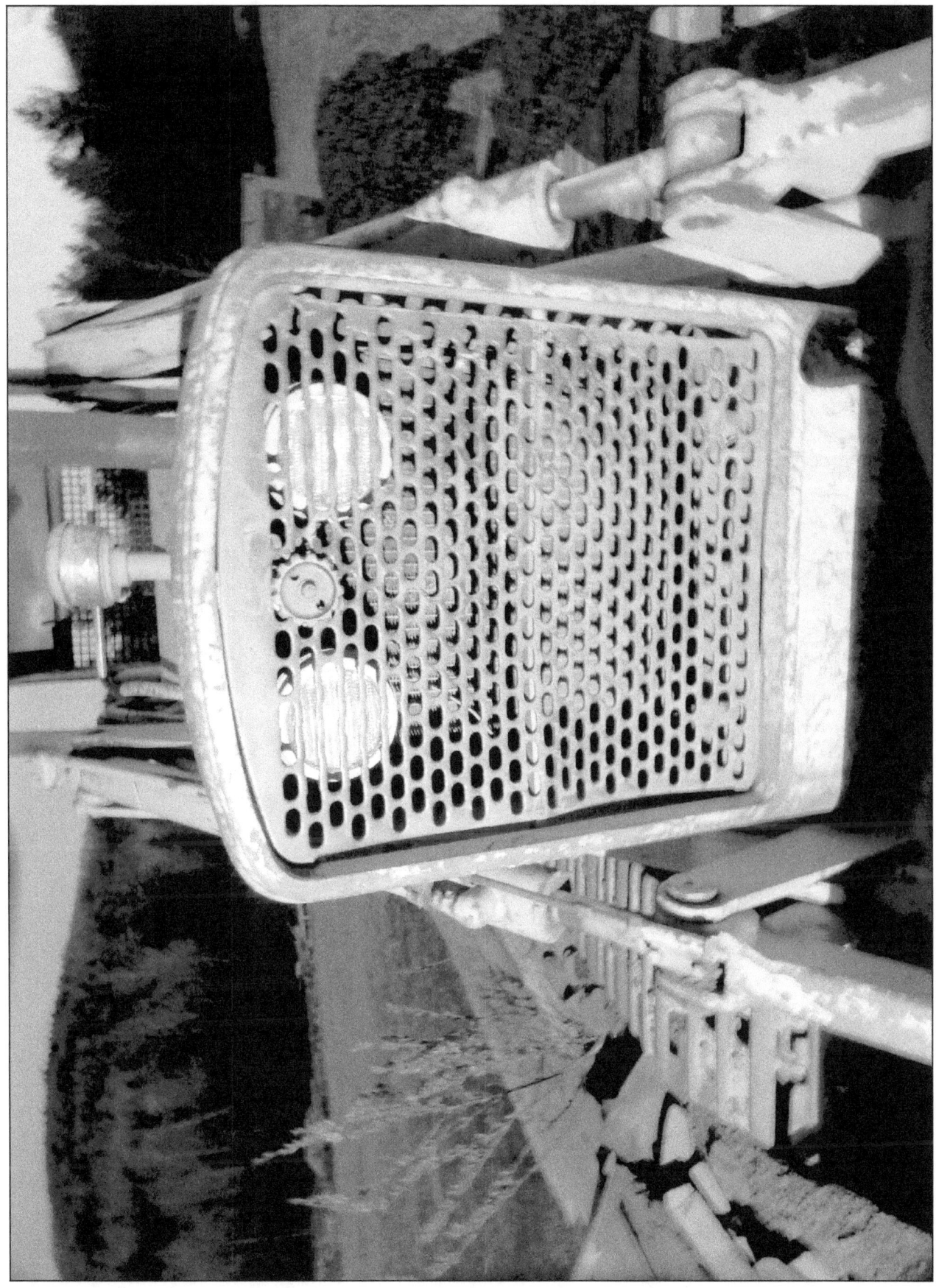

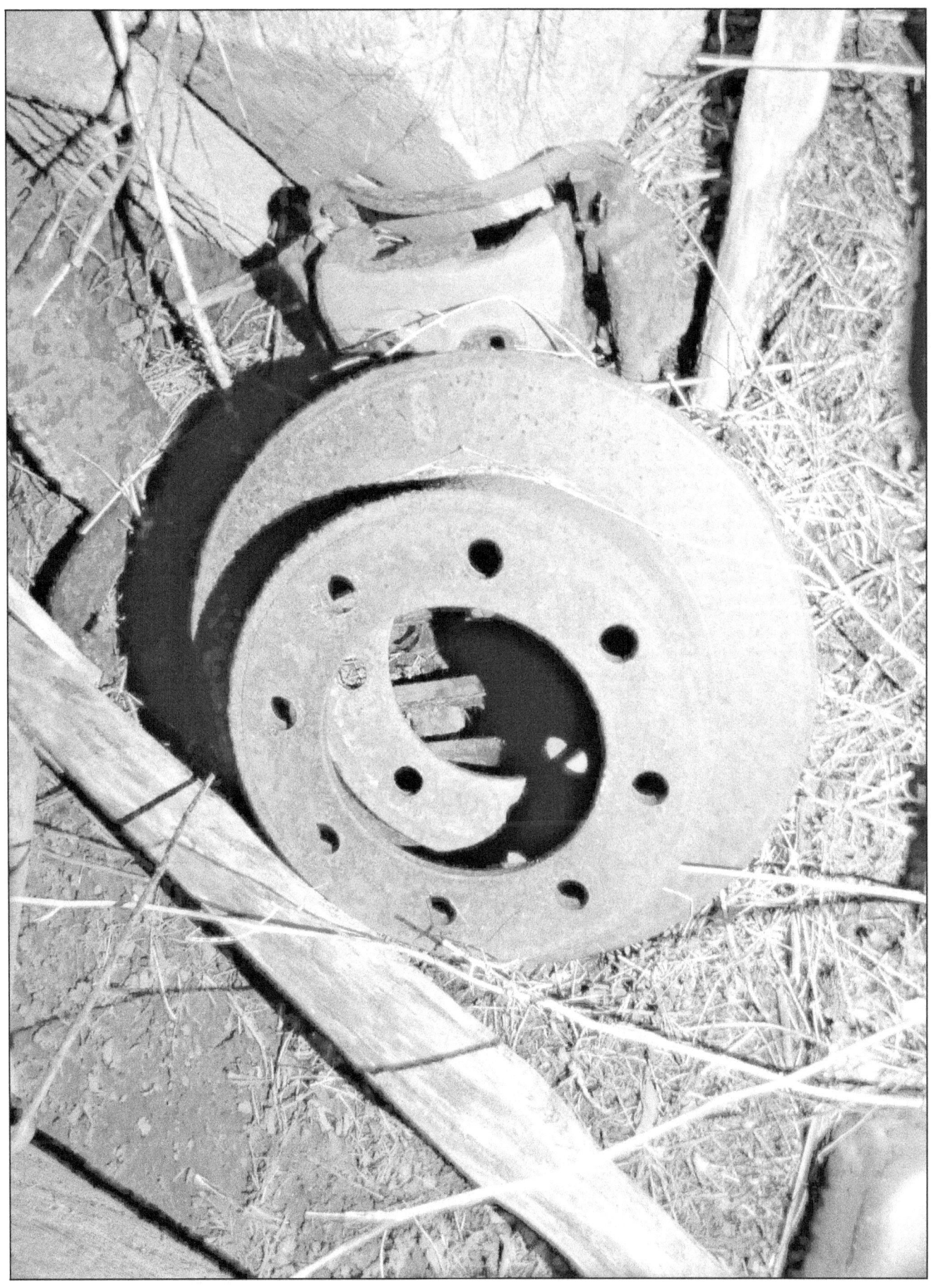

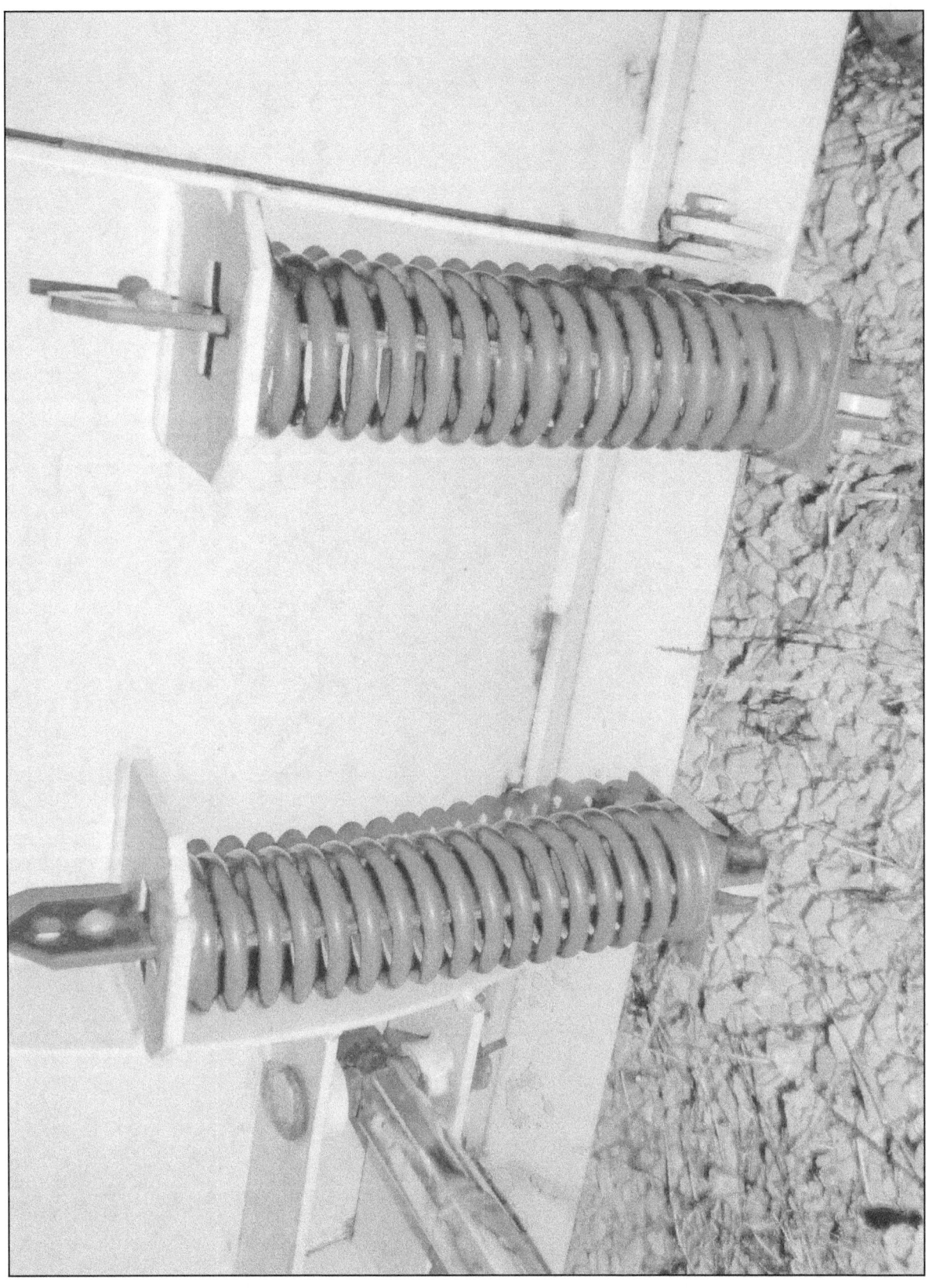

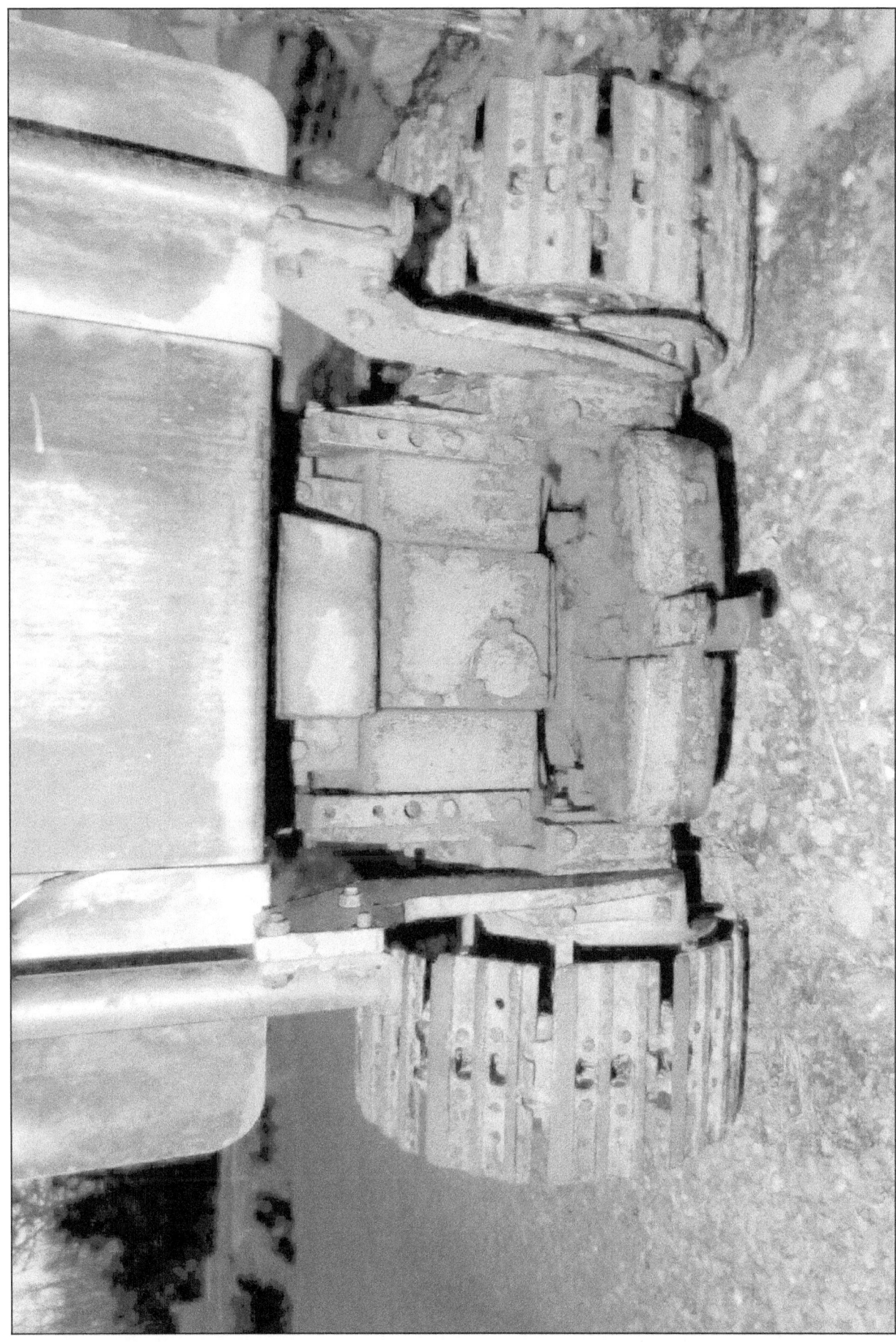

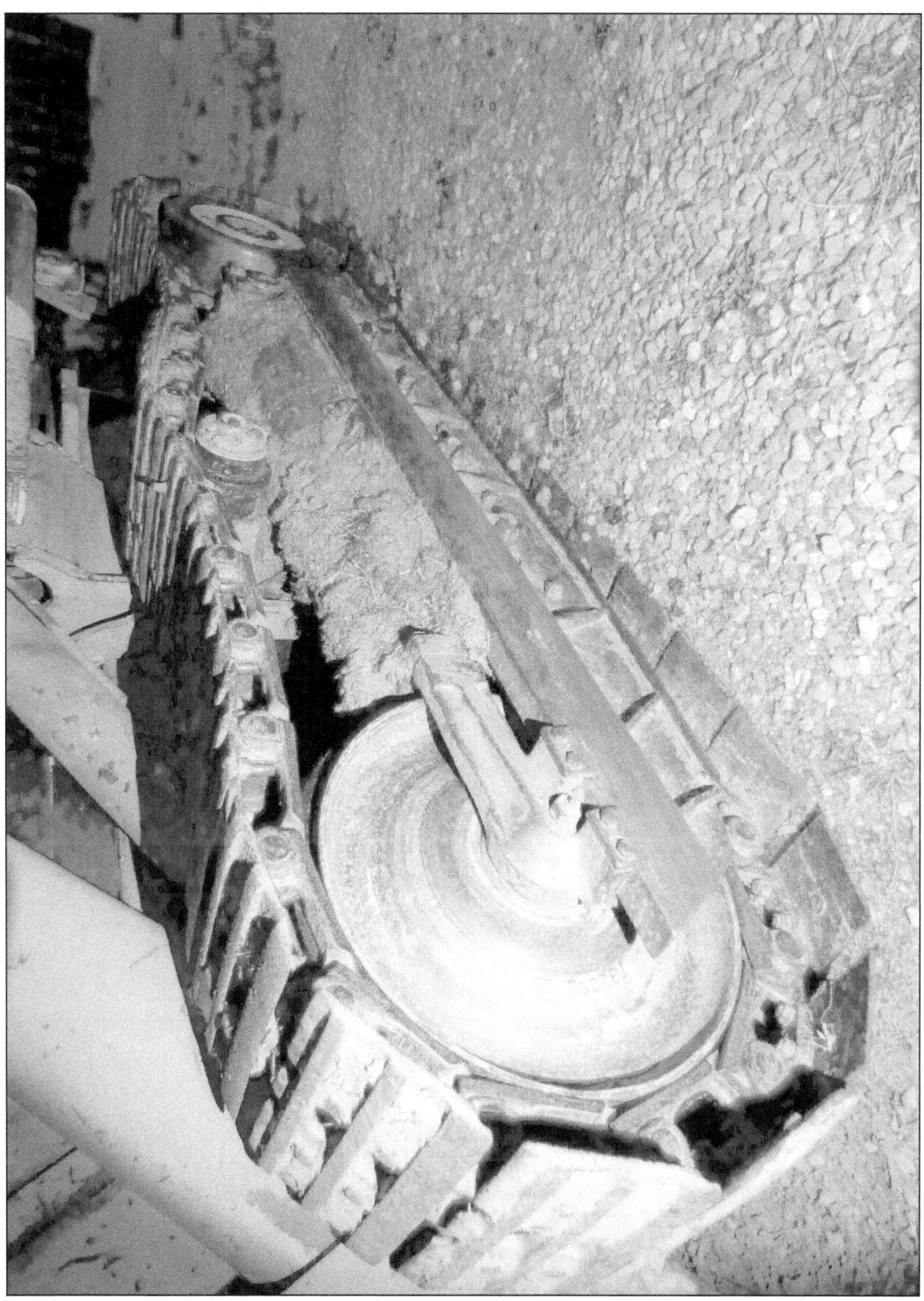

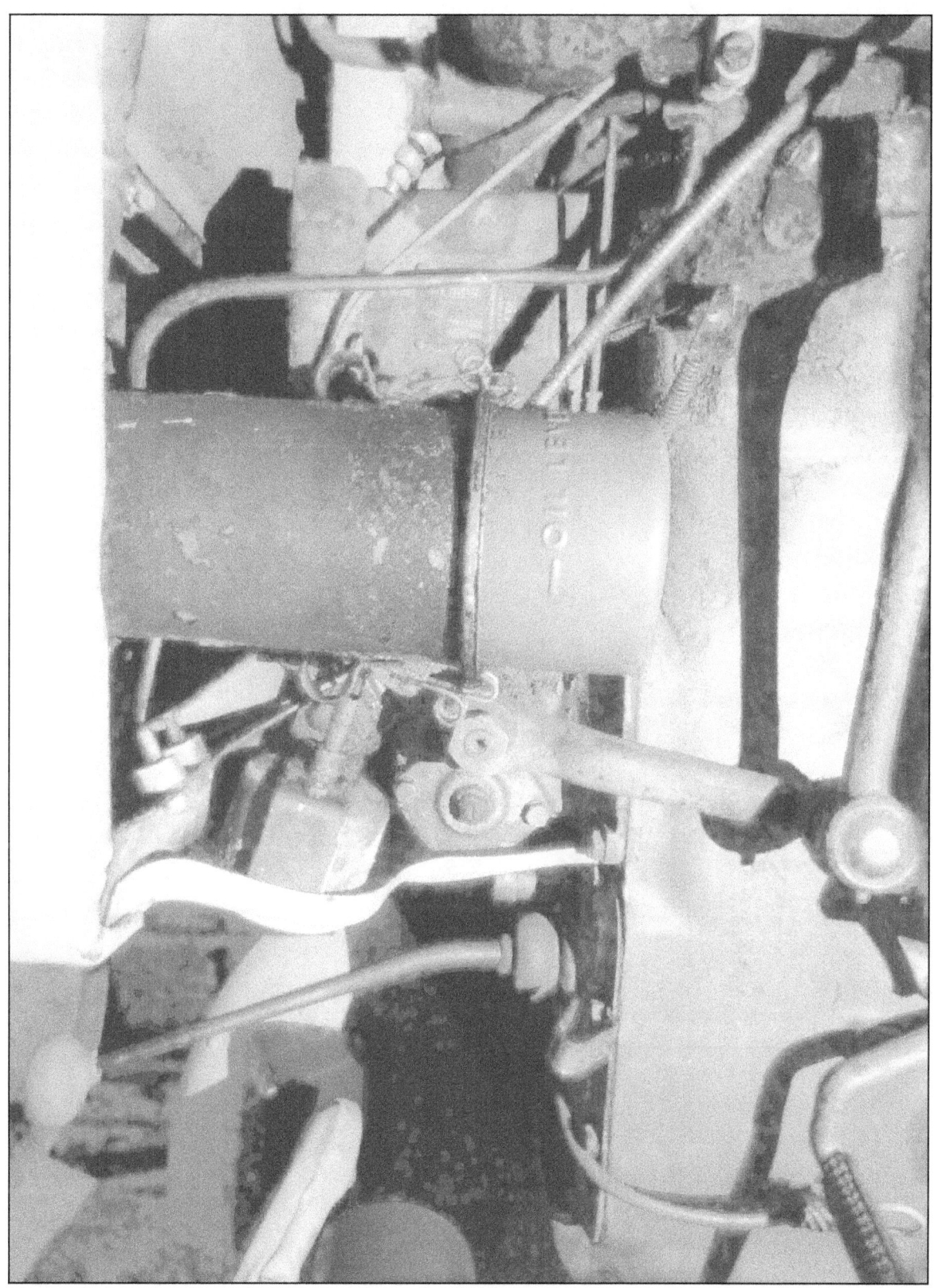

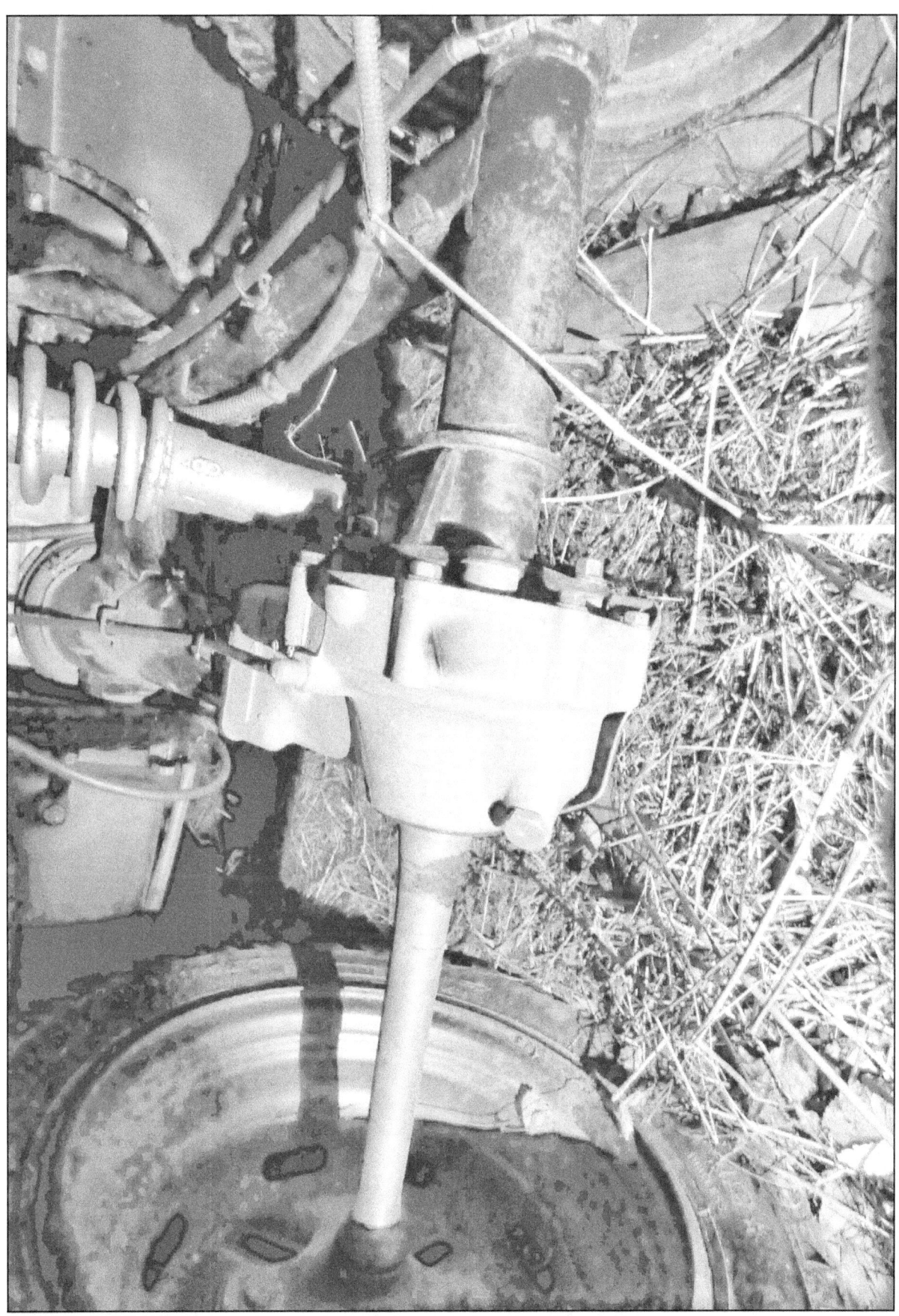

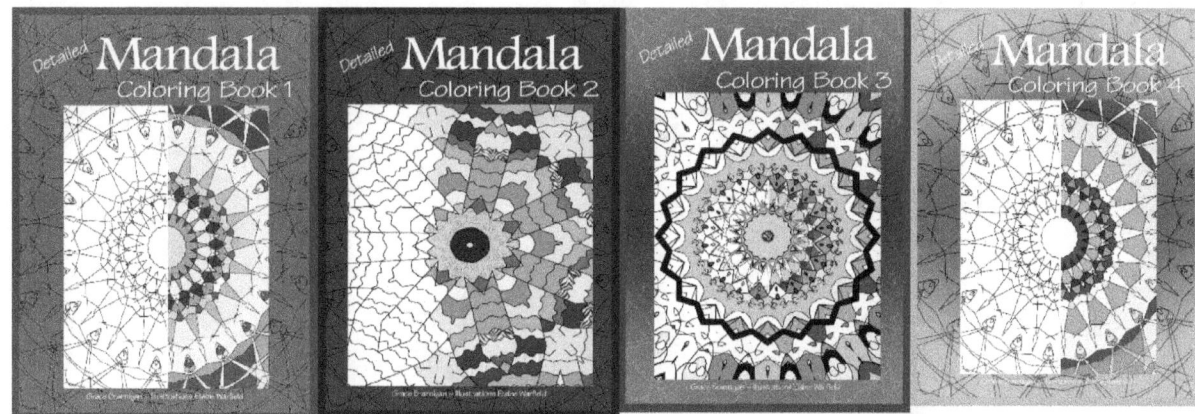

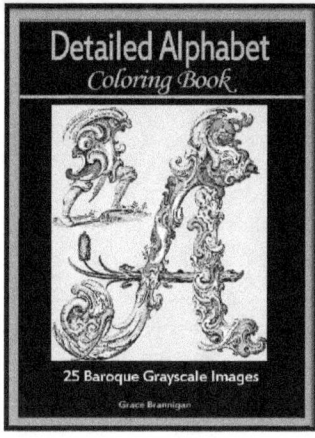 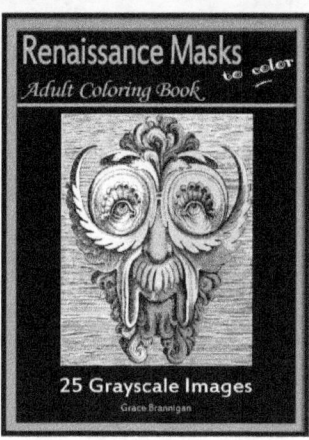

I hope you enjoyed coloring these grayscale images of Wheels, Cogs, Gears and Chains. Thank you for purchasing. Please go back to where you bought this book and leave feedback. It really helps the authors and potential buyers. Check out my website for all my coloring books!

Facebook: Coloring Books For Adults Info

Website: http://www.ColoringBooksForAdults.info

Twitter: @ColoringAdults

YouTube Channel with videos of all books and images

Grace Brannigan Author

www.ingramcontent.com/pod-product-compliance
Lightning Source LLC
Chambersburg PA
CBHW080723190526

45169CB00006B/2500